Teaching the Ten Themes of
Social Studies

MIDDLE SCHOOL

By

Ron Wheeler

Illustrations by

Tom Heggie

Published by Frank Schaffer Publications
an imprint of

McGraw-Hill
Children's Publishing

Credits
Author: Ron Wheeler
Illustrations: Tom Heggie

McGraw-Hill
Children's Publishing

A Division of The McGraw-Hill Companies

Published by Frank Schaffer Publications
An imprint of McGraw-Hill Children's Publishing
Copyright © 1996 McGraw-Hill Children's Publishing

Send all inquiries to:
McGraw-Hill Children's Publishing
3195 Wilson Drive NW
Grand Rapids, Michigan 49544

Teaching the Ten Themes of Social Studies—Middle School
ISBN: 0-7647-0011-1

Introduction

Teaching the Ten Themes of Social Studies is filled with teaching activities to help middle-level students comprehend the intricate web of relationships that link people with one another and their world. The book is organized around the 10 themes that make up the framework for the curriculum standards for social studies. These standards were developed and approved recently by the National Council for the Social Studies, which is the primary organization in the field. The standards focus on content from American and world history and the social science disciplines of sociology, anthropology, psychology, geography, government, and economics. The 10 themes that form the basis for the units in this book are the following:

- Culture

- Time, Continuity, and Change

- People, Places, and Environments

- Individual Development and Identity

- Individuals, Groups, and Institutions

- Power, Authority, and Governance

- Production, Distribution, and Consumption

- Science, Technology, and Society

- Global Connections

- Civic Ideals and Practices

All of the units include a variety of highly motivational activities that will sharpen your students' thinking about social studies. Specifically, each unit contains background notes for the teacher, performance expectations for students, teaching activities, a list of key teacher and student resources, reproducible student information sheets about the themes, and reproducible student activity sheets for independent study.

Can I really understand my own culture? Will the past shape my future? Why do I act and think the way I do? How can I make a difference in my community? *Teaching the Ten Themes of Social Studies* gives students an opportunity to find some of the answers to these important questions and others through gathering data and active investigation. The units in the book are designed to be student-friendly. There are plenty of hands-on experiences and links to real-life situations so students with diverse learning styles can achieve maximum success. Your students will enjoy high-interest activities like balancing a budget, shopping for bargains, designing a robot, creating a culture, searching for global-local connections, and many, many more.

Teacher Tips

Without a supportive classroom environment, it is easy for students new to theme-based learning to get off on the wrong foot. The specific ideas and activities contained in this book will be more effective if they are implemented in a positive classroom environment that provides opportunities for students to exchange points of view and investigate meaningful problems. Some things you can do to foster this environment are listed below.

- Let students identify and investigate their own problems and questions related to the theme.

- Use cooperative learning strategies that let students work together on theme-based problems.

- Invite people from the community into the classroom to share their perspectives on the theme.

- Encourage each student to make a special contribution to the study of the theme that draws on his or her unique talents.

- Have students keep journals in which they can record their reflections about their theme-based studies.

- Incorporate art, music, dance, and drama into the lessons.

- Use still and video cameras to keep a visual record of students' performance and projects.

- Use a variety of strategies to evaluate student progress, including collections of the students' work (portfolio assessment).

- Let students give and receive peer tutorial instruction.

- Send a note to parents about the thematic unit and involve parents in students' learning.

- Provide opportunities for independent study.

- Decorate the classroom attractively to highlight the theme.

- Show that you are interested in the theme by being an enthusiastic teacher.

- Create a reward structure to acknowledge positive individual and group behavior.

- Make certain each student knows that you believe he or she can be successful.

Culture

CHAPTER 1
Culture

Note to the Teacher: *Culture* is an all-encompassing concept. It refers to the myriad of feelings, beliefs, and habits that an individual shares with other members of society. To understand the concept of culture, students need to analyze its many aspects, such as language, family, education, religion, government, and technology. Because the United States is so ethnically diverse, students need to explore the range of cultural possibilities and then "see" those possibilities in relation to their own particular culture or way of life.

Unit Goal: The purpose of this unit is to help students explore the concepts of culture and cultural diversity, apply skill in processing and applying information, and express creative abilities.

Materials: This unit includes the following resources: teacher and student bibliographies, teaching activities on culture, a reproducible information sheet containing facts on culture, and reproducible student activity sheets for independent study.

RESOURCES

For Teachers:
Southern Poverty Law Center. *Teaching Tolerance.* (biannual magazine available at no charge to educators) 400 Washington Ave., Montgomery, AL 36104.

For Students:
Carter, Jimmy. *Talking Peace: A Vision for the Next Generation.* New York: Dutton Children's Books, 1993.

Catalano, Julie. *The Mexican Americans.* New York: Chelsea House, 1988.

Meltzer, Milton. *The Black Americans: A History in Their Own Words.* New York: T. Y. Crowell, 1984.

Meltzer, Milton. *The Jewish Americans: A History in Their Own Words.* New York: T. Y. Crowell, 1982.

Tames, Richard. *Islam.* London: Batsford, 1985.

Traub, James. *India: The Challenge of Change.* New York: Messner, 1985.

A Concept of Culture
Teaching Activities

Performance Expectations: Students will compare cultures, analyze different cultural perspectives, and examine contributions to the development and transmission of culture.

Preparation: Make individual copies of the information sheet "An Example of Culture," and the "Create a Culture," "Canadian and American Cultures," "Cultural Change," and "Cultural Diffusion" student activity sheets.

Introduction

To introduce the concept of culture, bring a screwdriver or some other common tool to class. Have students identify tools they can use. Ask them to discuss how they learned to use the tools. Explain that using technology is one aspect of culture. After students read the information sheet, have them compare the Muslim way of life with their own culture. Encourage students to consider possible reasons why cultures, or ways of doing things, differ both within and across societies.

Create a Culture (page 5)

Students should enjoy creating imaginary cultures. To help them focus on the task, ask them to locate their made-up cultures in real geographic regions. After they specify the types of climate, major land forms, and kinds of resources for their regions, it should be easier for students to create descriptions of the jobs and lifestyles of the people. Let students share their created cultures with the class. Probe students' understanding of the relationship between culture and environment.

Canadian and American Cultures (page 6)

To help students discover cultural differences and similarities, provide them with a variety of reference books that contain information about the history, climate, population, economy, government, and immigration policies of Canada and the United States.

Cultural Change (page 7)

Because of all the modern technological advancements, the rate of change is greater today than ever. After students complete the activity sheet, let them identify additional inventions that have caused great changes in the way people live. Have students use string and index cards to make a time line of the inventions. Discuss which inventions, in the students' opinion, were the most important in history.

Cultural Diffusion (page 8)

The spread of objects and ideas from one place to another provides a fascinating story about the development and transmission of culture. To help students visualize cultural diffusion, let them trace the spread of tobacco, silk, glass, coffee, paper, and rubber from culture to culture on individual world maps.

An Example of Culture

Imagine the following futuristic scenario: You have joined the Peace Corps, and you are going to live and work for two years in a Muslim country. You know that Muslims are followers of the religion of Islam. A quick check in the encyclopedia tells you that Islam is one of the world's largest religions. (There are over 1 billion followers worldwide and Muslims form the majority population of many countries.) You also learn that although there is great diversity among Muslims, Islam is more than just a religion—it is a whole way of life; it is a *culture*.

It is our culture that tells us what to think and believe and how to act. Muslims believe that God's teachings were revealed to the Prophet Mohammed, a seventh-century Arab. These teachings were written down by Mohammed's followers in the Koran, or holy book. The Koran has affected the Muslim way of life in many basic areas, including the following:

Language: Arabic is the sacred language of the Koran. Muslims believe that followers of Islam, regardless of their native language, should memorize important passages of the Koran in Arabic.

Architecture and Art: Out of respect for the supreme authority of God, Muslims do not generally use human and animal images in their architecture and art. Instead, Muslims tend to use abstract symbols and geometric patterns to decorate buildings, books, and other objects. Calligraphy, consisting of highly stylized Arabic script, is also a popular art form.

Dress: The Koran calls for modesty in dress. In some Muslim countries, women are required to cover their faces with veils and their legs with tunics or trousers when going out in public.

Family: The family is very important in Islam. A Muslim family often includes grandparents, uncles, aunts, and cousins.

Food and Drink: The eating of pork and drinking of alcohol are forbidden.

Politics: There is no separation between religion and government in traditional Muslim countries.

Muslims believe their world view is perfectly natural and correct. For most Americans, however, a different way of doing things seems normal and right. All humans have to learn their culture, but you cannot really *understand* your own culture unless you can compare it to other ways of doing things. Cultural understanding is especially important for Americans, even if they never leave their native country. In our ethnically diverse society, appreciating our differences can lead us to this important insight: beneath the surface, we are more alike than different.

Create a Culture

Culture refers to many aspects of living. It includes the items below. Use your imagination to create a culture. Describe your imaginary culture on the blank spaces provided.

The name of my culture is _____.

Language (What are some commonly used words?)

_____

_____

Food (How is food gathered and/or produced?)

_____

_____

Family (Who are the members of a typical family?)

_____

_____

Shelter (Draw a picture of a typical family's shelter.)

Government (What is the political organization like?)

_____

_____

Dress (Draw a picture of the types of clothing worn by the people.)

Religion (What are the religious beliefs of the people?)

_____

_____

Education (What do the young learn from their elders?)

_____

_____

Canadian and American Cultures

Canada and the United States have much in common. But each nation also has its own unique history and traditions. On the Venn diagram below, list aspects of Canadian culture and American culture that are shared, aspects of American culture not shared with Canada, and aspects of Canadian culture not shared with the United States. Consult a reference book if necessary. To get you started, an example is provided for each section.

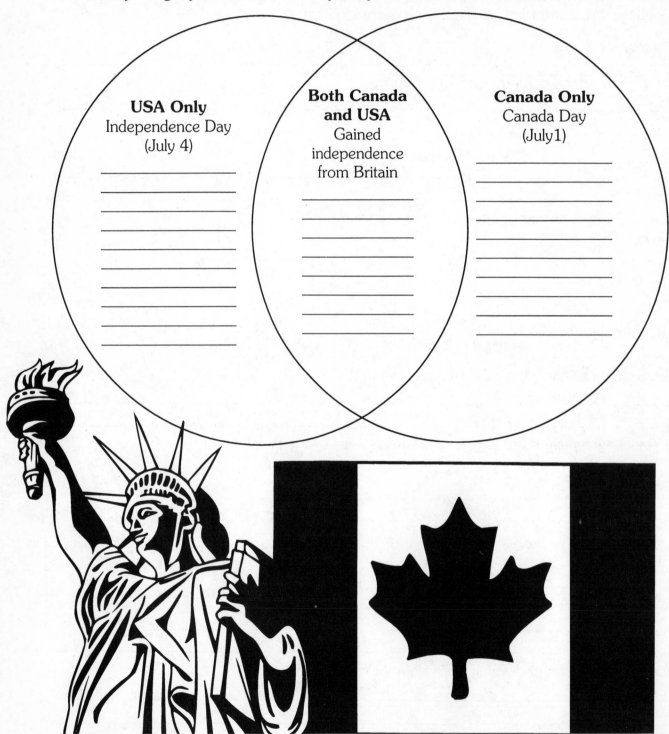

USA Only
Independence Day
(July 4)

Both Canada and USA
Gained independence from Britain

Canada Only
Canada Day
(July 1)

Cultural Change

The amazing inventions listed below have caused, and will continue to cause, great changes in culture everywhere. On the blank spaces provided, briefly explain how each of these inventions helped change people's relationships with family and friends, work patterns, access to information, contact with strangers, and education. Then, on a separate sheet of paper, answer this question: What impact have these inventions had on American culture? Speculate on how further technological advances will affect the future.

Jet Plane

_____
_____
_____
_____

Personal Computer

_____
_____
_____
_____

Communications Satellite

_____
_____
_____
_____

Fax Machine

_____
_____
_____
_____

Television

_____
_____
_____
_____

Cultural Diffusion

Cultural diffusion refers to the spreading of culture from one place to another. For example, after tobacco was introduced into Europe from America in the late 1500s, the habit of smoking spread rapidly across Europe. Listed below are some items commonly found in American society that were borrowed from other cultures. Use library resources to find out where they originated. Then write a brief history of each item on the spaces provided.

Silk

_____

_____

_____

_____

Cotton

_____

_____

_____

_____

Glass

_____

_____

_____

_____

Coffee

_____

_____

_____

_____

Paper

_____

_____

_____

_____

Rubber

_____

_____

_____

_____

Cultural Diversity
Teaching Activities

Performance Expectations: Students will consider the implications of cultural diversity and examine why individuals and groups respond differently to situations and circumstances on the basis of shared values and beliefs.

Materials: Make individual copies of "Cultural Alphabet Soup," "Combating Stereotypes," and "Cultural Dynamics."

Cultural Alphabet Soup (page 10)
There is a tendency to overgeneralize about people, thereby concealing important distinctions among cultural groups. For example, lumping people under broad categories like "Asians" or "Europeans" makes it harder to perceive the cultural differences between, say, Thai and Japanese, or Scots and Irish. Searching for the names of Indian cultural groups will give students a sense of the great diversity that exists within the category "Native Americans." Encourage students to supplement their in-depth written reports on a specific Native-American group with examples of the tribe's art, music, and dance (they can check the school and community libraries for illustrated books, as well as audio and video tapes).

Combating Stereotypes (page 11)
Many people know how it feels to be the victims of stereotypes. Unfortunately, too many people have let stereotypes influence their attitudes about ethnic groups and other populations in American society. As students observe and analyze how various groups are portrayed on television, they should gain a keener awareness of the cultural messages created by the media. If students have access to channels that run old sitcoms from the 1950s and 1960s, they can compare role models and stereotypes on TV then and now.

Cultural Dynamics (page 12)
Over time, cultures change. Some critics of contemporary American society argue that our values have been undermined by poverty, drugs, negative role models, and the breakup of the family. They say that instead of cultural cohesion, a divisive "anything goes, do-your-own thing" attitude predominates. Some social scientists observe that the core values of teenagers are surprisingly similar to those of their parents. Let students discuss their opinions about the quote by the football coach. Are any of the coach's values and attitudes revealed in the quote? If so, are his values valid? As extensions of this activity, students can write and illustrate classified ads for the position of teacher or coach. Other extensions would be for students to interview their parents or other older people to ascertain whether they believe America's values are changing, or to write essays expressing their opinions about the values for which America should stand. In addition, have students identify cultures around the world that adhere to values different than those of the coach.

Cultural Alphabet Soup

Native American and *Indian* are general terms that refer to a rich variety of distinct cultural Native-American groups. From A (Abenaki) to Z (Zuni), the list of Native-American groups is a long one. The U.S. government officially recognizes more than 540 Native-American tribes. Use encyclopedias and other sources to help you track down the names of any 20 of these tribes. Then write the name of each tribe on the cultural alphabet soup can shown below. To get you started, the two tribes named above are already listed for you on the can. On a separate sheet of paper, describe one Native-American tribe in detail. Research the following topics about your group: customs, traditions, technology, location, and effects of European contact.

Combating Stereotypes

A *stereotype* is an oversimplified or inaccurate mental image about a whole group of people that is based on inadequate information. Television shows and commercials reflect a variety of opinions about and values found in American culture. Next time you watch TV, keep a record of how the following groups are presented. What images are TV viewers receiving? Do the images reflect the diversity of cultures or are they stereotypes?

Women

_____
_____
_____
_____

Men

_____
_____
_____
_____

Teenagers

_____
_____
_____
_____

The Elderly

_____
_____
_____
_____

African Americans

_____
_____
_____

Hispanics

_____
_____
_____
_____

Cultural Dynamics

Read the quote below, and then answer the questions that follow.

> I teach values like dedication, toughness, courage, and stamina. My players must have the ability to endure pain and hardship, and I push them to the limit. I demand obedience. When I explain something to them, they must give me their complete attention. I insist on direct eye contact. When I make an important point, I want them to blink or nod!

Would you want this person to be your coach or teacher? Why or why not?

_____

_____

_____

_____

_____

Does American culture value the same qualities as this coach?

_____

_____

_____

_____

_____

Time, Continuity, and Change

CHAPTER 2
Time, Continuity, and Change

Note to the Teacher: To gain a historical perspective, students must transcend the "here and now" and expand their sense of time and space. If students can draw upon history as a resource for dealing with problems that confront them today, they will be more likely to see the connection between themselves and time, continuity, and change.

Unit Goal: The purpose of this unit is to help students explore the ways human beings view themselves in and over time, to let them apply skills in processing and applying information, and to express creative abilities.

Materials: This unit includes the following resources: teacher and student bibliographies, teaching activities on history, a reproducible information sheet containing facts about history, and reproducible student activity sheets for independent study.

RESOURCES
For Teachers:
Editors of American Heritage. *A Sense of History: The Best Writing From the Pages of American Heritage.* New York: American Heritage, 1985.

Tindall, George Brown. *America: A Narrative History.* (2 vols.). New York: W.W. Norton, 1988.

For Students:
Books
Carey, Helen H. and Judith E. Greenberg. *How to Use Primary Sources.* New York: Franklin Watts, 1983.

Carruth, Gorton. *What Happened When: A Chronology of Life and Events in America.* New York: Perennial Library, 1989.

Magazines
Cobblestone: The History Magazine for Young People. (Published monthly, except June, July, and August, by Cobblestone Publishing, 7 School Street, Peterborough, NH 03458).

Software
Where in America's Past Is Carmen Sandiego? Novato, CA: Broderbund Software, 1992. (This computer game turns American history into a detective adventure.)

Making History

Teaching Activities

Performance Expectations: Students will use historical concepts to analyze change and continuity both within and across cultures.

Preparation: Make individual copies of the information sheet "Time, Continuity, and Change," and the "Personal History," "The Good Old Days," and "Historical Time" student activity sheets.

Introduction

To get students thinking about the past and the role of the historian, ask them to recall some activity in which they all participated. (Just about any activity, like working on a special project, listening to a lecture, or taking a field trip will do. If something especially notable happened during the activity, so much the better.) Encourage students to describe the particular event as vividly as possible. As the students talk, write their descriptions on the chalkboard. After the "history" of the event is recorded, challenge students to evaluate their work. In reconstructing the past, did they use a variety of sources (eyewitnesses, in this case)? Did they check the credibility of the sources? Are students certain their history is accurate? After students have finished their discussion, let them read the information sheet "Time, Continuity, and Change," which develops the idea that everyone needs a "sense of history."

Personal History (page 17)

This activity helps students realize that history is not just about the long ago and far away—it can be up close and personal, too. Have volunteers share their personal histories with the class. Do students have similar histories? How did they decide which events to include?

The Good Old Days (page 18)

Before students conduct their interviews, ask them to predict whether or not elderly people will say the "good old days" were better than today. Students can also hypothesize about how that age group will answer the questions about leisure-time activities, chores, special days, and school and community life. When the interviews are completed, students can contrast their own lives with the older generation's.

Historical Time (page 19)

As students apply their math skills, they will gain a better temporal perspective of historical events. Students will begin to "see" the proper relationship of events to one another through time. As a whole-class activity, you might want to create large thematic time lines on the chalkboard or paper. Let each 12-inch segment on the line equal a 100-year span. Challenge students to add events and their dates to the time line. Of course, to locate the proper points, students will first have to do the calculations and measurements correctly. Some possible themes for time lines are the rise of civilizations, the development of transportation systems, and the growth and development of colonial systems.

Time, Continuity, and Change

What happened to you yesterday? Think about all the things that occurred from the time you awoke until bedtime. What did you learn yesterday that might help you today? Now think about all the things that have happened in the world since you were born. Have any of those past events affected your life? Will they shape your future? Without knowledge of past events, you would have no sense of time, continuity, or change. In a nutshell, you would have no sense of history.

A sense of history can help you comprehend the present and imagine the future. But before it can be useful, history must be as accurate as possible. When you read about the Revolutionary War, the Civil Rights Movement, or any other event in history, you want to know what really happened. Without a diligent search for truth, what passes for history may be little more than "a fable agreed upon," to quote Napoleon, or "bunk," as Henry Ford liked to bluntly put it. The careful procedures used by historians to record history had their origins in Greece over 2,000 years ago. Before the careful recording of history began, knowledge of the past was based mostly on made-up myths and folklore. Historians are always looking for solid evidence to back up what they say. They are also on the lookout for *bias*, the greatest enemy of truth. Bias in history can take many forms, including exaggeration, over-generalization, emotion-laden words, uninformed opinions, and imbalance.

Developing a sense of history takes more than just memorizing facts. You must sense the presence of history in your own life. First and foremost, history is about people. American history is chock-full of famous people—like Davy Crockett, Abraham Lincoln, Amelia Earhart, and Martin Luther King, Jr.—who lived and died heroically. But American history is also about millions of other men and women whose names were not recorded in books, but who, nonetheless, participated vigorously in the important events of their times. They were the common folk—builders and traders, slaves and immigrants, laborers and artisans, farmers and clerks, scholars and apprentices, soldiers and preachers. While it might be hard to relate our own lives to those larger-than-life paragons of history, we all can try to live up to the pioneering spirit of the many who came before us.

Each generation has a duty to tell the lessons of the past to the next generation. Many of those lessons are about success and accomplishment, but others are about failure and unrealized dreams. Simply possessing knowledge of history, however, is not enough. There also must be a deep interest in how the lessons of history can be applied today. When you study history, ask yourself these two questions: "What does this knowledge tell me about the nature of people and societies?" and "How can I use this knowledge to make the right decisions for myself and society?"

Personal History

You are making history every day! Each of us has a personal history. Think about all of the things that have happened to you since you were born. Now choose some significant events to include in the personal time line below. In the spaces provided, write a brief description and the date of each of the events so that they are arranged in order of their occurrence. The first significant event, your birth, is done for you. Just fill in the date. For your last entry, describe an event that occurred recently.

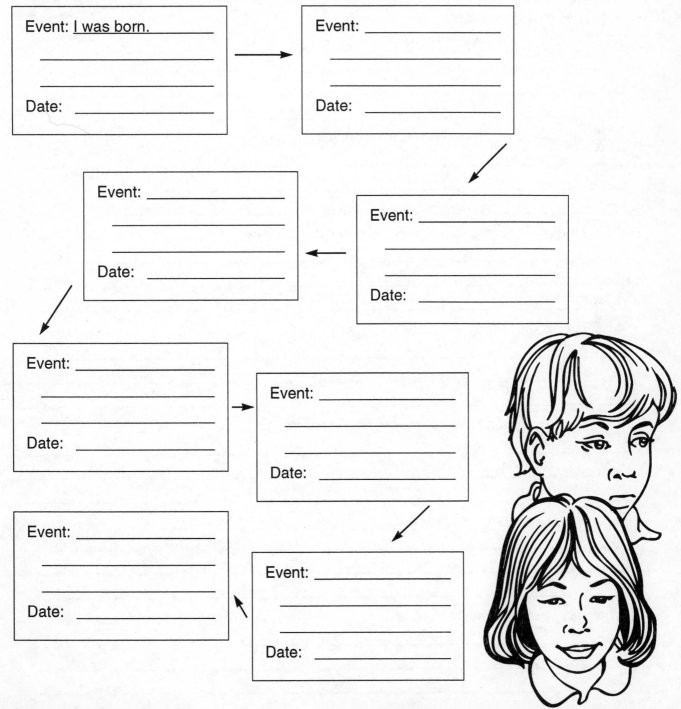

Event: I was born. _____

_____

_____

Date: _____

Event: _____

_____

_____

Date: _____

Event: _____

_____

_____

Date: _____

Event: _____

_____

_____

Date: _____

Event: _____

_____

_____

Date: _____

Event: _____

_____

_____

Date: _____

Event: _____

_____

_____

Date: _____

Event: _____

_____

_____

Date: _____

The Good Old Days

Some older people say they yearn for the "good old days," which they usually define as the time period when they were growing up and going to school. Your assignment is to interview an elderly person. You want to learn about the life of that person when he or she was your age. If possible, record the interview on a cassette tape. Ask the questions below. Use the blank spaces to summarize the person's responses to the questions.

When and where were you born?

_____

_____

What important lessons did you learn from your family?

_____

_____

What kinds of leisure-time activities did you participate in?

_____

_____

What chores did you do at home?

_____

_____

What special days and events did your family celebrate?

_____

_____

What was your school day like?

_____

_____

What was your community like?

_____

_____

Historical Time

The time span between Columbus' arrival in America in 1492 and the election of Bill Clinton as President of the United States in 1992 was 500 years. Your assignment is to complete the time line that shows the chronology (or order of occurrence) of the events listed randomly below. First, you need to use library resources to determine the year in which each of the events occurred. Then, to make the time line more meaningful, you are going to arrange the events on the line in a way that reflects their proper time relationship to one another.

Cornwallis surrendered at Yorktown.
The French and Indian War began.
The first humans walked on the moon.
The Civil War ended.
The Lewis and Clark expedition began.
The first African slaves came to Virginia.
The California Gold Rush began.
de Soto discovered the Mississippi River.
An earthquake destroyed San Francisco.

The time span of 500 years is represented by the vertical line at the right. Each segment of the line equals a 100-year span. Find the approximate points on the line that correspond to the correct chronological sequence for the events listed above. Then label each point with the matching event and its date.

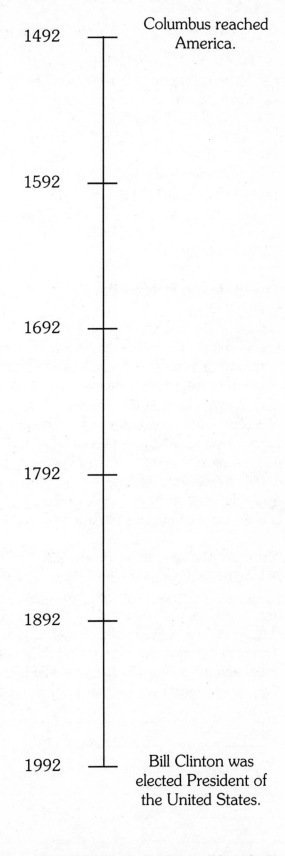

Name _____

1492 — Columbus reached America.

1592 —

1692 —

1792 —

1892 —

1992 — Bill Clinton was elected President of the United States.

Doing History
Teaching Activities

Performance Expectations: Students will demonstrate an understanding of historical perspective, use processes of inquiry, and use historical data to make informed decisions about public issues.

Preparation: Make individual copies of the "The Meaning Behind the Facts," "Multiple Perspectives," "The Historian's View of History," and "Using History" student activity sheets.

The Meaning Behind the Facts (page 21)

Before students complete the activity sheet, engage them in a discussion of the *meaning* of events. Ask students whether or not the statement "Columbus reached the New World in 1492" is worth knowing. Challenge them to give reasons for their views. Make certain students are aware that Columbus' voyages led to destruction of Native American cultures, establishment of European colonies, and enslavement of millions of Africans.

Multiple Perspectives (page 22)

After students complete the activity, assign them to small groups (three or four per group) and let them share their answers. Based on their research, did they find that Americans during this period held different views about slavery? Challenge students to identify important issues that divide people today.

The Historian's View of History (page 23)

Most accounts of President Kennedy's assassination state that he was shot by a lone gunman, Lee Harvey Oswald, whose motives remain unknown. By comparing sources on the assassination, students should see that, although accounts of the same events may be very similar, no two histories are exactly the same. While the major themes and events of history tend not to change, each historian will tell the story from his or her own viewpoint.

Using History (page 24)

This activity gives students an opportunity to focus on current issues of concern to them. Before students begin their investigations, remind them to be open-minded to new information about the issues. Discuss how personal bias could interfere with weighing or evaluating the evidence.

As an extension, pose this question, "Which inventions and scientific ideas have had the most significant effects on history?" Have students explore the effects of technology on these civilizations: Mesopotamia, Ancient Egypt, Ancient China, Ancient Greece, the Roman Empire, nineteenth-century Britain, and twentieth-century United States.

The Meaning Behind the Facts

History is more than remembering lists of *events and dates*.
Historians want to know the *meaning* of events. For example,
almost everyone knows that Columbus arrived in America in
1492, but fewer people understand the full significance of that
epic voyage, which changed the world. Columbus' discovery of
the New World led to disagreement between Spain and Portugal,
the destruction of Native American cultures, the establishment of
European colonies, and the enslavement of millions of Africans.
Some other important events and their dates are listed below.
What do these events *mean*? Use your research skills to discover
their significance; then write down your findings in the spaces
provided.

1. The Pilgrims' landing at Plymouth (Massachusetts) in 1620

_____

_____

2. The signing of the Declaration of Independence in 1776

_____

_____

_____

3. The introduction of Eli Whitney's cotton gin in 1793

_____

_____

_____

4. The election of Abraham Lincoln as president of the United States in 1860

_____

_____

_____

5. America's decision to drop the atomic bomb on Hiroshima and Nagasaki in 1945

_____

_____

_____

6. The breakup of the Soviet Union in 1991

_____

_____

_____

Multiple Perspectives

In reconstructing and interpreting events, historians consider a variety of perspectives. *Perspective* refers to how an event is perceived and interpreted from different points of view by participants. Your assignment is to sample some perspectives on slavery in the United States during the period leading up to the Civil War. Your research question can be stated as follows: What were the perspectives on slavery of various prominent individuals and groups in U.S. society before the Civil War? Use classroom and library sources to piece together information about the perspectives of the people and groups listed below. (Actually, this assignment will help you make some hypotheses, or educated guesses, about possible answers to the question above. To test the accuracy of your hypotheses, you will need to examine as much information as possible, which is exactly what a historian would do.)

Harriet Beecher Stowe and her book *Uncle Tom's Cabin* published in 1852
Perspective:

_____

_____

_____

Source(s) used: _____

The Supreme Court and the Dred Scott case in 1857
Perspective:

_____

_____

_____

Source(s) used: _____

William Lloyd Garrison and his newspaper, *The Liberator*, founded in 1831
Perspective:

_____

_____

_____

Source(s) used: _____

Henry Clay and his "Compromise of 1850"
Perspective:

_____

_____

_____

Source(s) used: _____

The Historian's View of History

History is not about *everything* that ever happened. When writing a book, each historian must decide which facts to include and which to exclude. The historian must also interpret the facts so that the meaning of events is clear. The investigation into the assassination of President John F. Kennedy, who was slain in Dallas, Texas, has produced much controversy. Although most interpretations say that a lone assassin killed the president, some argue that more than one person was involved. Find three source books (you can choose from biographies, history textbooks, encyclopedias, and other books) that describe the events surrounding the death of President Kennedy. Then summarize what each of the three sources had to say about the assassination in the spaces provided below.

The Assassination of President John F. Kennedy

Name of source book: _____

Author(s): _____

Summary: _____

_____

_____

_____

_____

Name of source book: _____

Author(s): _____

Summary: _____

_____

_____

_____

_____

Name of source book: _____

Author(s): _____

Summary: _____

_____

_____

_____

_____

Using History

What is your stand on crime, drugs, health care, housing, discrimination, affirmative action, foreign aid, child abuse, education, military spending, free trade, taxes, welfare, student loans, or the space program? Those are just some of the many public issues facing America today. Choose one of the above or another current issue of concern to you to investigate in depth. Then gather facts and concepts drawn from history that are related to the issue to help you better understand it. Use the space below to express your opinion on the issue. Make certain your written statement includes the following three elements: (a) a clear, specific statement of your position on the issue, (b) a strong, logical argument that draws on historical information, and (c) a conclusion that summarizes the argument. Include a list of sources consulted in the development of your statement.

_____

_____

_____

_____

_____

_____

_____

_____

_____

_____

_____

_____

_____

_____

_____

_____

_____

_____

_____

_____

_____

People, Places, and Environments

CHAPTER 3
People, Places, and Environments

Note to the Teacher: For many students, the most exciting portion of their school day is when they get a chance to apply a geographic view to a particular life situation. That is because, of all the disciplines taught in the classroom, only geography allows students to see the "big picture"—that is, to see the web of dynamic relationships that exist among people, places, and environments across the surface of the planet Earth. The geographic view is both local and global. It is about metropolitan traffic patterns and world shipping routes, a community's weather and global climate, city maps and satellite images of Earth.

Unit Goal: The purpose of this unit is to help students explore the relationships among people, places, and environments, apply skill in processing and applying information, and express creative abilities.

Materials: This unit includes the following resources: teacher and student bibliographies, teaching activities on geography, a reproducible information sheet containing facts about people, places, and environments, and reproducible student activity sheets for independent study.

RESOURCES
For Teachers:
Bednarz, Sarah W., et. al. *Geography for Life: National Geography Standards 1994*. Washington, DC: Geography Education Standards Project, 1994.

Boorstin, Daniel J. *The Discoverers*. New York: Random House, 1983.

For Students:
Books
Curtis, Neil, and Michael Allaby. *Planet Earth*. New York: Kingfisher Books, 1993.

Thackray, John. *The Earth and Its Wonders*. New York: Larousse, 1980.

Magazines
National Geographic World. (Published by National Geographic Society, Washington, D.C.)

Software
Where in the World Is Carmen Sandiego? Novato, CA: Broderbund Software.

Geographic Connections
Teaching Activities

Performance Expectations: Students will compare and contrast ecosystems, examine geographic factors that influenced the rise of ancient civilizations, and use maps.

Preparation: Make individual copies of the information sheet "People, Places, and Environments" and the "Exploring Ecosystems," "The Geography-Civilization Connection," and "World Landmarks" student activity sheets.

Introduction

To stimulate students' visual thinking about the planet Earth, challenge them to make free-hand drawings of their state, the nation, or the world from memory. They can use circles, squares, triangles, and other simple shapes to represent places on their maps. When they have finished, let them compare their geographic representations with maps in atlases and almanacs. Which features of a place did they include? Which did they leave out? Do the students' maps show an understanding of relative location, size, and shape? Discuss the types of geographic information represented by points, lines, symbols, and color on maps. Let students read the information sheet "People, Places, and Environments," which discusses why a geographic perspective is necessary in today's interconnected world.

Exploring Ecosystems (page 29)

Before students complete the activity sheet, discuss the characteristics of the ecosystem in which they are located. Into which ecosystem does the local area fall? How have people changed the natural conditions found in the local ecosystem?

The Geography-Civilization Connection (page 30)

After students have completed their investigations of the four ancient civilizations, it should become clear to them that all four places shared one very important characteristic—they all were situated in river valleys. The flooding of the rivers made the soils fertile. These conditions allowed small hunter-gatherer groups to evolve into large, complex, agricultural-based civilizations.

World Landmarks (page 31)

Let students discuss local and regional landmarks before doing the activity sheet. Ask interested students to create a bulletin board display of world landmarks and their locations, using pictures and maps that they have gathered. As a culminating activity, try the following cooperative project. Divide the class into groups of three or four students. Let each group create a one- or two-minute television commercial that promotes one of the landmarks as a tourist attraction. The groups can create skits, oral presentations, jingles, songs, and other devices for their commercials.

People, Places, and Environments

People often ignore the obvious. The Earth stretches before us as far as the eye can see, and the sun is the most striking spectacle in the sky, yet neither one gets the attention—or the respect—it deserves. Among all the known planets, only Earth has special characteristics that nourish life. The sun's warm rays are the power source for the planet's climates, as well as for its many *ecosystems,* which consist of living things interacting with their environment. For millions of years, only natural processes such as weather, erosion, earthquakes, and volcanic activity, influenced Earth's interacting systems. But now, thanks to modern technology, humans can—and do—interfere with nature in many ways. As a result of this meddling, the planet is in trouble.

Many forms of human activity put our planet at risk. Farming, fishing, ranching, logging, mining, and manufacturing have led to the destruction of wetland, forest, prairie, ocean, and other ecosystems. Economic development worldwide has released billions of pounds of pollutants into the air, water, and land. Habitat destruction has threatened hundreds, perhaps thousands, of species of plants and wildlife around the globe and places many species under immediate threat of extinction. Earth is also becoming a more crowded place. Each year, the world's population increases by about 93 million. With more and more people competing for control of the planet's surface, the need for global cooperation and cultural understanding becomes imperative.

Geography can help us understand and solve these problems. A geographic view of the world gives meaning to the arrangement of things in space and reveals how people, places, and environments are interconnected. Geography deals with questions like the following: "How do people, places, and environments differ?" "How are goods and ideas exchanged across regions of the world?" and "How is the physical environment changed by human activities?" Because of global interdependence, people everywhere are, in a sense, neighbors. Good neighbors must accept responsibility for how their actions affect others. Local actions can have far-reaching consequences. For example, the demand for new housing in communities throughout the United States creates a tremendous demand for plywood and other wood products that contributes to the destruction of tropical rain forests, which, in turn, reduces living space for a multitude of species and possibly affects the global climate.

What is your favorite place or environment? Is it somewhere in the mountains or along a sandy beach? Is it in a bustling city or a quiet country town? Is it far away or in your own back yard? Once your thoughts start to extend beyond yourself, you can journey through your imagination to anywhere on Earth. But before you depart, keep this in mind: the trip will be greatly enriched by the geographic knowledge you take along with you.

Exploring Ecosystems

An *ecosystem* is made up of living things interacting with their environment in a certain place. Different ecosystems are listed on the left side of the chart below. To learn more about them, gather information from library resources and fill in the chart. Then use the chart information to respond to the following question: In what ways have people changed the natural conditions found in ecosystems? Write your response on a separate sheet of paper.

Ecosystem	Locations	Climate	Plants	Animals	Problems
Temperate Broadleaf Forest					
Needleleaf Forest					
Prairie					
Desert					
Rain Forest					
Mountain					
Ocean					

The Geography-Civilization Connection

Why did all of the world's earliest civilizations begin where they did? Did they all have certain geographic characteristics in common? Research each of the civilizations listed below. Then, on the blank spaces, describe the geographic factors that contributed to each civilization's rise.

1. Mesopotamia

_____

_____

_____

_____

2. Ancient Egypt

_____

_____

_____

_____

_____

3. Indus Valley of South Asia

_____

_____

_____

_____

_____

4. Huang Valley of North China

_____

_____

_____

_____

_____

_____

World Landmarks

Ten of the world's most famous landmarks are described below. Your task is to use library resources to identify and locate them. Then write the name of the landmark on the blank space next to the description. Finally, write the number that corresponds with each landmark to show its proper location on the map.

_____ 1. Colorful fish swim among the world's largest chain of coral reefs in this underwater wonder.

_____ 2. As you sail toward beautiful Guanabara Bay, first the mountains and then the skyline of this South American city come into view.

_____ 3. Reaching to the heavens, this peak, which is the world's highest, is a splendor to behold.

_____ 4. More than a mile deep and over 200 miles long, this spectacular gorge in the U.S. Southwest is awe-inspiring.

_____ 5. In the heart of Africa, this 355-foot waterfall is named for a British queen.

_____ 6. Cutting through the desert, this river, which is the world's longest, once nourished the pharaohs and their people.

_____ 7. A variety of animals and more than 200 geysers can be found in this national park, which is America's oldest.

_____ 8. This sacred landmark is not only Japan's highest mountain, it is also its most well-known symbol.

_____ 9. Unique wildlife and natural splendors await you when you journey to this rain forest, which is the world's largest.

_____ 10. When viewed from Waikiki Beach in Honolulu, this ocean-front mountain is a spectacular sight.

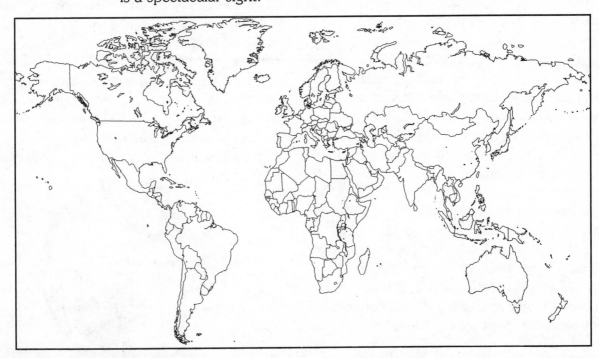

Local and Global Views
Teaching Activities

Performance Expectations: Students will use maps, describe geographic patterns, analyze settlement patterns, and explore the relationship between cultural values and ways people use their environment.

Preparation: Make individual copies of the "Earth Facts," "Capital Coordinates," "Mystery Nations," and "A Geographic Checklist for Your Community" student activity sheets.

Earth Facts (page 33)
Let students use reference books to help them fill in the missing facts about the planet Earth. As an extension to this activity, challenge students to gather additional facts about Earth. Make certain they can document the sources for the facts they collect and encourage them to use a variety of resources. They can include books, encyclopedias, atlases, almanacs, magazines, and newspapers.

Capital Coordinates (page 34)
Use this activity to build students' skills using latitude and longitude. Then have them work independently to find coordinates for other cities and/or countries. Later, let partners exchange and identify their coordinates.

Mystery Nations (page 35)
To give students practice recognizing the shapes of the continents and countries of the world, create an interactive bulletin board. Laminate outline maps of the following major land areas: North America, with separate maps for the Caribbean islands and Greenland; South America; Europe; Australia, with a separate map for New Zealand; Antarctica; Africa, with a separate map for Madagascar; West Asia (often called the "Middle East"); Central Asia; South Asia; East Asia, with a separate map for Japan; and Southeast Asia. Cover the bulletin board with blue paper. Put the laminated map pieces in a large container located on or near the board. Let individuals use push pins to arrange the land areas properly on the board to create a recognizable world map.

A Geographic Checklist for Your Community (page 36)
Have each student select a question (or an aspect of a question) on the activity sheet for independent study. Encourage students to gather information from a variety of community sources. You also might want to provide students with information you have collected. Students can draw maps of the community that show the spatial distribution of industries, parks, shopping centers, libraries, emergency-care facilities, fast-food restaurants, schools, and other services. What are the patterns of land use in the community? What do students' investigations of their community tell them about the values of the residents, both past and present?

Earth Facts

There are a number of interesting facts about the planet Earth contained in the passage below. Your task is to use library resources to locate the missing information. Then, fill in the blanks with the correct facts.

With a diameter of _____ (a) miles, Earth is the _____(b) largest planet and the _____ (c) planet from the sun. Earth's average distance from the sun is _____ (d) million miles. Moving at 18½ miles a second, the planet makes one _____ (e) about the sun in 365¼ days and makes one _____ (f) on its invisible axis every 23 hours and 56 minutes. Every June 21, the sun's direct rays are at the Tropic of _____ (g). On the equinoxes, the sun's direct rays are at the _____ (h). Earth's atmosphere is composed mainly of nitrogen, argon, and _____ (i). About _____(j) percent of the planet's surface is covered by water.

A globe is a very accurate representation of the planet Earth. Positions on the globe's surface are measured by imaginary lines. Lines that run through the poles are called _____(k). Lines that run parallel to the equator are called _____ (l).

Capital Coordinates

The latitude and longitude coordinates for 10 world capital cities are listed below. Refer to an atlas to locate and identify the capitals. Write the names of the capitals and their countries in the spaces below. Then fill in the coordinates for five other capitals and identify them.

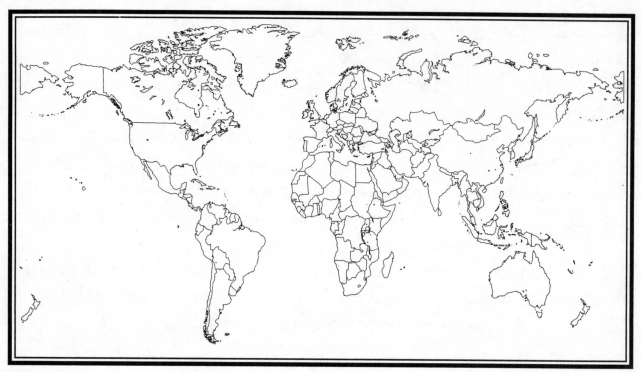

Latitude	Longitude	Capital, Country
1. 38° N	24° E	_____
2. 40° N	116° E	_____
3. 52° N	13° E	_____
4. 6° S	107° E	_____
5. 51° N	0° E	_____
6. 19° N	99° W	_____
7. 56° N	38° E	_____
8. 41° S	175° E	_____
9. 39° N	77° W	_____
10. 45° N	76° W	_____
11. _____	_____	_____
12. _____	_____	_____
13. _____	_____	_____
14. _____	_____	_____
15. _____	_____	_____

Name _____

Mystery Nations

Can you recognize the nations shown below by their shapes? To be certain, find each country on a world map. (Hint: numbers 2, 4, 5, 6, and 7 are very large nations.) Write the names of the nations on the blank spaces below.

1. _____

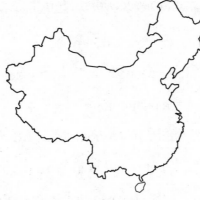

2. _____

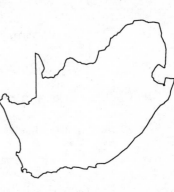

3. _____

4. _____

5. _____

6. _____

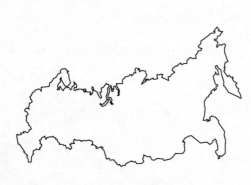

7. _____

8. _____

9. _____

A Geographic Checklist for Your Community

To learn more about the geographic aspects of your community, stay abreast of the local news and keep informed about community leaders. Here are some questions to investigate.

- ➤ Does your community have a development plan?

- ➤ Do roads, streets, and intersections handle traffic adequately?

- ➤ Are parks and recreation areas adequate?

- ➤ Are there green areas to buffer residential areas from roads and noise?

- ➤ Are historical areas in the community being preserved?

- ➤ Do factories in your community release pollutants into the air, water, or land?

- ➤ Are street crossing locations for pedestrians safe and adequate?

- ➤ Is access to sidewalks, rest rooms, shops, offices, and other buildings adequate for disabled persons?

- ➤ Are sidewalks in good condition?

- ➤ Do streets, roads, and parking areas have adequate lighting?

- ➤ Does your community have bike and walking trails?

- ➤ Does your community suffer from noise pollution?

- ➤ Are fire, health, and other emergency services available throughout the community?

- ➤ Does your community have laws that control the location and size of business signs?

- ➤ How do your community's zoning laws protect your community?

- ➤ Are there nature centers or preserves for observing plants, birds, and animals?

- ➤ Are there areas for sitting, playing, boating, fishing, and gardening?

- ➤ Where are industries, parks, shopping centers, libraries, fast-food restaurants, schools, and other services located?

- ➤ Are there volunteers who donate time and materials to build playgrounds for children, to repair the homes of the poor, elderly and disabled, or to perform other community services?

Individual
Development and Identity

CHAPTER 4
Individual Development and Identity

Note to the Teacher: Psychologists tell us that subject matter and instruction need to be combined in ways to help middle-level students develop curiosity, confidence, and competence. This unit helps close the gap between subject matter and students. It focuses on the developmental needs of every student by tying subject matter to the personal and political choices students will need to make in their lives.

Unit Goal: The purpose of this unit is to help students examine their individual development, apply skill in gathering and processing information, and express creative abilities.

Materials: This unit includes the following resources: teacher and student bibliographies, teaching activities, a reproducible information sheet containing facts on individual development, and reproducible student activity sheets for independent study.

RESOURCES

For Teachers:
Chase, Stuart. *The Proper Study of Mankind.* New York: Harper, 1963.
Maslow, Abraham H. *Toward A Psychology of Being.* Princeton, NJ: Van Nostrand, 1962.

For Students:
Greene, Constance C. *Monday I Love You.* New York: Harper & Row, 1988.

Hill, David. *See Ya, Simon.* New York: Dutton Children's Books, 1992.

Tolan, Stephanie S. *Pride of the Peacock.* New York: Charles Scribner's Sons, 1986.

Ure, Jean. *The Most Important Thing.* New York: William Morrow, 1986.

Ure, Jean. *The Other Side of the Fence.* New York: Delacorte Press, 1988.

Me, Myself, and I
Teaching Activities

Performance Expectations: The student will relate capabilities, motivation, personality, and perception to individual development and personal growth, and analyze personal and school-based factors that are related to identity and personal change.

Preparation: Make individual copies of the information sheet "Individual Development and Identity," and the "Individuality Inventory," "My Everyday Life," "Changing a Bad Habit," and "Development Quiz" student activity sheets. Also, provide each student with an orange. (You can use lemons instead, but do not mix the two.)

Introduction
To introduce students to the concept of "individuality," follow these procedures: (1) give each student an orange; (2) let each student carefully study his or her orange for a few minutes; (3) collect all the oranges and put them together on the floor or on a table; and (4) challenge each student, in groups of five or six at a time, to find his or her own orange. Most students should be able to identify their oranges and relate this activity to the idea that each person has characteristics that make him or her unique and special.

Individuality Inventory (page 41)
After students silently read the information sheet "Individual Development and Identity," discuss the key ideas. They should then be ready to complete this activity sheet, which focuses on the connection between individual

development and the following factors: capabilities, motivation, personality, and perceptions.

My Everyday Life (page 42)
To get students thinking about the activity, disclose some things about a typical day in your own life. After they complete their accounts, let individuals in groups of four or five students take turns reading their papers aloud.

Changing a Bad Habit (page 43)
This activity will be more fun if you participate, too. To introduce the activity, tell the class about a bad habit of yours; then encourage students to suggest ways for you to break the habit. When the activity is finished, you may be among those who broke their bad habits.

Development Quiz (page 44)
If possible, help your students administer the quiz to all of the students in the school. That way, you will have a complete picture of students' perceptions of the school's ability to meet individual development needs. Students can tabulate the data and then create tables and charts to display the results of their findings. What conclusions can students draw from the results? If the quiz uncovers areas of concern, you can involve students in a discussion of what might be done about them.

Individual Development and Identity

"If I were you,..." How many times have you said those very words as you prepared to impart some friendly advice to someone? The truth, of course, is that neither you nor anyone else can be another person. You can only be yourself. Discovering your *identity*, or who you are, is an important part of growing up. As you get older, your concept of "self" changes. When you were a baby, feelings about yourself were associated with a small circle of people who were responsible for your welfare. Today, your horizon has expanded greatly, and your personal life is connected to people and ideas that span the globe and reach far back into time. Some factors that have influenced your individual development are described briefly below.

Social—Humans are social creatures. We are members of many groups. There are family, friendship, school, and work groups. We learn the many roles we play in society from the groups in which we belong. Think about some things you have learned to do well. Who taught you how to do those things?

Cultural—The ways people organize and use their environment are determined by their culture. *Culture* is a complex set of values, attitudes, and behaviors characteristic of a particular society. What are some cultural characteristics that you share with other Americans?

Historical—Each generation transmits cultural information about the past to the next generation. In our society, for example, the story of the struggle for freedom and equality has inspired young Americans to examine the present and work for social change.

Capabilities—Each of us is capable of learning new information and skills, and we all have hidden talents that are waiting to be discovered. To identify your capabilities, you must be open to new ideas and then be willing to test them out for yourself.

Motivation—Why do some people seem to achieve their goals while others do not? Successful people believe in themselves. They know they can learn from their mistakes, and they believe that if they keep trying, they eventually will accomplish the task.

Personality—How would someone who knows you well describe you? Would they say you are flashy or quiet, gloomy or jolly, shy or bold, serious or silly?

When it comes to personal characteristics, there is a tendency for young people to be too hard on themselves. Put-downs, whether from peers or self-inflicted, can damage the human spirit. Fortunately, pessimistic views can be changed into optimistic ones by thinking positively. Everyone wants to be with people who make positive, constructive comments. To show people you care, remember to build on their strengths, rather than focus on their weaknesses.

Individuality Inventory

Complete this inventory to learn more about yourself.

Capabilities: Some things that I
do well include

_____
_____
_____
_____
_____
_____
_____
_____

Motivation: Some things that
make me want to try harder
include

_____
_____
_____
_____
_____
_____
_____

Me

Personality: Some adjectives
that describe me include

_____
_____
_____
_____
_____
_____
_____

Perception: Some things I like
about myself include

_____
_____
_____
_____
_____
_____
_____

Name _____

My Everyday Life

On the spaces provided below, write a brief autobiographical account of a typical day in your life. Include information about your attitudes and habits, your diet, your school work, and your leisure time.

_____

_____

_____

_____

_____

_____

_____

_____

_____

_____

_____

_____

_____

_____

_____

_____

_____

_____

_____

_____

_____

_____

_____

_____

_____

Changing a Bad Habit

Everyone has at least one bad habit he or she would like to break. Such habits might include tossing dirty clothes on the floor, not listening to others, eating too much junk food, or being too critical of others, to name a few. Identify a bad habit you want to break; then follow these steps. Use the chart below to keep a daily record of the habit for two weeks. Try not to engage in the bad habit, but if you do, make a mark on the record sheet for each time it happens, day by day. Also make a note of where and why you engaged in the habit. At the end of the two-week period, analyze the results. On the back of this page, make two lists, a list of reasons why you think you engage in the bad habit and another list of reasons why you should give up the habit. The more you concentrate on trying to break the habit, the more likely you are to succeed. Good luck!

The bad habit I want to break is _____

Week 1

Sunday	Monday	Tuesday	Wednesday	Thursday	Friday	Saturday	Total

Notes:

Week 2

Sunday	Monday	Tuesday	Wednesday	Thursday	Friday	Saturday	Total

Notes:

Development Quiz

Below are factors that affect individual development. Circle the score that best describes your school.

3—very true for your school
2—somewhat true for your school
1—not at all true for your school

At my school, there are ample opportunities for students to

1. develop leadership skills   3   2   1

2. express individual opinions   3   2   1

3. develop positive relationships with one another   3   2   1

4. share ideas and skills with one another   3   2   1

5. influence decision-making   3   2   1

6. receive recognition   3   2   1

7. develop creative talents   3   2   1

8. work together cooperatively to achieve a common goal   3   2   1

9. engage in intellectually challenging activities   3   2   1

10. resolve interpersonal conflicts peacefully   3   2   1

You and the World
Teaching Activities

Performance Expectations: Students will relate personal identity to social, cultural, and historical contexts, and identify ways world, national, ethnic, and regional cultures influence individual development.

Preparation: Make individual copies of the "Family Values," "Circles of Culture," and "Ties to the Past" student activity sheets.

Introduction
Read aloud sections of Daniel DeFoe's book *Robinson Crusoe*—the story of a ship-wrecked Englishman who managed to survive alone on an island. Have students speculate about what it might be like to be cut off from the influence of other persons for a long period of time.

Family Values (page 46)
This activity will provide an opportunity for students and their family members to share their beliefs and values with one another. After students identify their families' values, they can share them with other students in small groups of five students. Have the groups decide which values are checked most often. Are some values shared by all or most families?

Circles of Culture (page 47)
The Northern American culture circle will include words, customs, ideas, and material items from Native American cultures (i.e., a respect for nature and canoeing), the American frontier culture (i.e., a belief that opportunities were unlimited), and other previous cultural eras, as well as from contemporary culture (e.g., TV, rock music, and cars). Encourage students to consult family members and other people in the community about ethnic and regional cultural characteristics. Be prepared for items that might appropriately be assigned to more than one circle. For example, "jazz" could be included inside the "Ethnic" circle as well as in the "Northern American" circle. A powerful way to conclude this activity is to create an extra large "Circles of Culture" diagram to hang on the wall of the classroom. Students can make their individual contributions to the diagram by taking turns writing their cultural descriptions inside the appropriate circles.

(Note: For an insightful analysis of "cultural rings" and the culture concept, see *The Proper Study of Mankind* by Stuart Chase.)

Ties to the Past (page 48)
This activity will help students see the connections between themselves and the lives of four famous figures from American history. Encourage students to read biographies that bring the historical characters to life. As an extension to this activity, have each student assume the role of one of these historical figures and portray some aspect of his or her life to show how it relates to the student's life.

Family Values

The family is the most important transmitter of values from one generation to the next. How does your family see itself in relation to the values listed below? (If you would like, you can add other values to the bottom of the list.) In the columns under "Family Members," have each family member place a check mark in the appropriate boxes to indicate the values each member of your family believes are most important to have. (There are columns for up to five family members, including yourself.) If possible, get the whole family together to discuss the values and then reach consensus on the most important values to have. This can be recorded in the last column on the right.

Your Family Values	You	_____	_____	_____	_____	Family Consensus
Honesty						
Courage						
Obedience						
Hard Work						
Loyalty						
Fairness						
Success						
Friendliness						
Compassion						
Generosity						
Wealth						
Intelligence						
Responsibility						
_____						
_____						

Circles of Culture

As suggested by the diagram below, you are surrounded by many circles of culture that shape your values, attitudes, and behavior. Some of the most basic aspects of your way of life come from the world's earliest non-Western civilizations (located in Asia and Africa) and from Western civilizations (including Greek, English, and French). Some of their cultural contributions are listed inside the *Non-Western* and *Western* circles. What customs, ideas, and material things come from each of the three inner circles? Use library resources and personal knowledge to describe characteristics that belong in the *Northern American* (historical and present-day), *Regional* (based on what is distinctive about your region) and *Ethnic* (based on your ethnic identity) circles. These characteristics might include food preferences, resource use, tools, music, art, occupations, leisure-time activities, inventions, and beliefs. Write the characteristics for each circle on a separate sheet of paper.

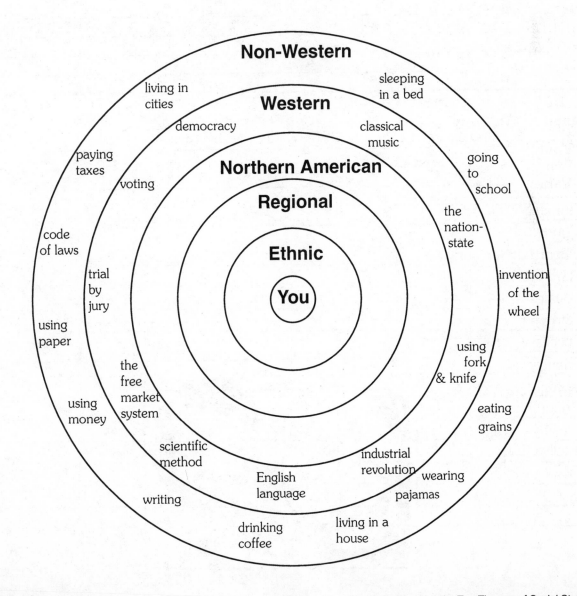

Ties to the Past

Research the lives of the four individuals from American history listed below. Then, in the spaces provided, describe an attitude, a skill, a habit, an interest, or a belief that you share with each of the historical characters.

Abraham Lincoln

_____
_____
_____
_____
_____

George Washington

_____
_____
_____
_____
_____

Susan B. Anthony

_____
_____
_____
_____
_____

Martin Luther King, Jr.

_____
_____
_____
_____
_____

Individuals, Groups, and Institutions

CHAPTER 5
Individuals, Groups, and Institutions

Note to the Teacher: In an age of transition, society must appear to middle-level students much like an unfamiliar road covered with both steppingstones and stumbling blocks. There are plenty of opportunities to find meaning and enjoyment, but there are also confusions and conflicts to overcome. This unit examines society and its many groups and institutions from the students' points of view.

Unit Goal: The purpose of this unit is to help students understand the interactions among individuals, groups, and institutions, apply skills in processing information, and express creative abilities.

Materials: This unit includes the following resources: teacher and student bibliographies, activities on individuals, groups, and institutions from multiple content areas, a reproducible student information sheet about the topic, and reproducible student sheets for independent study.

RESOURCES

For Teachers:

Johnson, David W., and Roger T. Johnson. *Learning Together and Alone.* Englewood Cliffs, NJ: Prentice-Hall, 1987.

For Students:

Atanasoff, Stevan E. *How to Survive As a Teen.* Scottdale, PA: Herald Press, 1989.

Peck, Lee A. *Coping With Cliques.* New York: The Rosen Publishing Group, 1992.

Rosen, Roger, and Patra McSharry (editors). *Street Gangs: Gaining Turf, Losing Ground.* New York: The Rosen Publishing Group, 1991.

Stevens, Sarah. *Cults.* New York: Crestwood House, 1992.

Stewart, Gail B. *Peer Pressure.* New York: Crestwood House, 1989.

Society and Me
Teaching Activities

Performance Expectations: Students will read the information sheet about individuals, groups, and institutions; understand concepts such as society, socialization, role, and status; and analyze group and institutional influences on people, events, and elements of culture.

Preparation: Make copies of the "Society and Me" information sheet and the "Understanding Society," "Individual Similarities and Differences," "Role and Status," and "Powerful Influences" student activity sheets.

Introduction

Write the word *society* on the chalkboard. Ask students to tell you what *society* means and list their definitions on the board. Help them classify the items on the list as examples of the following: groups (two or more people who share beliefs or values and have a sense of belonging, such as families, clubs, sports teams, and close friends), institutions (significant organizations in society, such as religious, educational, political, and economic), both, or neither. Introduce students to the "Society and Me" information sheet by asking students to read sections aloud. Help clarify their understanding and discuss their ideas about the material covered.

Understanding Society (page 53)

When students have finished reading the information sheet, they should be able to complete this activity sheet. Do students recognize sources of conflict between themselves and society?

Individual Similarities and Differences (page 54)

To better understand their roles in society, students need to analyze how they are like others. This activity sheet lets students make these important analyses by forming pairs and sharing their answers. Have students discuss the question "How are you like your partner?" Then let students individually respond to the question in writing.

Role and Status (page 55)

This activity sheet will familiarize students with two important concepts used by sociologists to analyze human behavior. Let them apply the two concepts to other social organizations such as a classroom or a club. Individuals perform multiple roles in society. Have the class list all the roles they perform currently and those to which they aspire in the future.

Powerful Influences (page 56)

Groups and institutions that affect people and events are the focus of this activity sheet. Help students realize how close groups and institutions are to their daily lives. Discuss the groups and institutions that influenced the event listed on the page.

Society and Me

Why do you act the way you do? What do you think and care about? Although every individual is unique, society is constantly influencing us to act in very similar ways. *Society* is a community of people who share common interests, traditions, and institutions. The way American society does things helps define us as a people. What would you choose as "examples" of our society? Would you include sitting down to turkey dinner on Thanksgiving Day, celebrating a friend's birthday, eating a hot dog at the ballpark, going on a trip to Disney World, or watching a popular television program? Would you include a common set of values that describe the good citizen, such as support of the law, a concern for the dignity of others, and participation in government? Learning to function in acceptable and predictable ways in society is called *socialization*. You are showing evidence of socialization when you do chores at home, attend school, and obey your teachers.

Ever since you were born, you have been part of a group. The most significant social group in your early years was comprised of your parents and/or other adults who provided you with food, shelter, and a sense of belonging. As you grow up, spending time with peers becomes increasingly important. You probably identify with many social groups in and out of school, including classes, teams, and clubs. If you are like most young people, however, you feel best when you are with your friends, to whom you look for advice and approval and with whom you share your concerns and hopes. In a poll of 8,000 young people (10- to 14-year-olds), three of the most troubling concerns were grades, looks, and popularity.

Growing up in our modern world is not easy. It is hard to concentrate on positive personal and social goals when the entertainment industry popularizes individuals and groups that promote violence, intolerance, drugs, drinking, and sexual misconduct. Sometimes it is difficult to "just say 'no' " when it appears that *everyone* is involved in self-destructive behavior. In America's increasingly violent society, young people are drawn to street gangs and criminal activity because the odds often seem stacked against them. The reasons they give for rejecting society's values include racism, poverty, hopelessness, missing family support, easy money, excitement, and peer pressure.

One of the biggest problems of growing up is dealing with two forces that often conflict. One force, which comes from outside, is based on society's needs. Society needs to regulate individual behavior and maintain the social system. The other force, which comes from inside, is based on personal needs. To reach their full potential, individuals must develop a sense of competence and responsibility, receive the support and recognition of significant others, and have the companionship and acceptance of friends. The challenge is learning how to satisfy those inner needs in ways that contribute to society and to your own good.

Understanding Society

After reading the information sheet "Society and Me," answer the following questions:

1. Define the two terms below:
   society:

   _____

   _____

   _____

   socialization:

   _____

   _____

   _____

2. The information sheet says that 10- to 14-year-olds worry about grades, looks, and popularity. Do you agree that those are important concerns? Why or why not?

   _____

   _____

   _____

3. Why do you think young people are increasingly drawn to self-destructive and criminal activities?

   _____

   _____

   _____

4. List some sources of conflict that can occur between society and the individual.

   _____

   _____

   _____

5. What are some of the characteristics that you like about your best friend or friends?

   _____

   _____

   _____

Individual Similarities and Differences

Who are you? How are you similar to and different from your classmates? Fill out the personal identification sheet below. Then pair up with another student and compare your responses. Together with your partner, make a list of the similarities and differences.

1. Describe a few things about your past.

   _____

   _____

2. What do you like to buy with your spending money?

   _____

   _____

3. Write down some adjectives that describe your personality.

   _____

   _____

4. List all the groups both in and out of school to which you belong.

   _____

   _____

5. List your favorite for each of the following items:

   dessert _____

   snack _____

   movie _____

   song _____

   singer _____

   politician _____

   place to go on vacation _____

   TV program _____

   color _____

   flavor of ice cream _____

   sandwich _____

   soft drink _____

   car _____

   sport _____

   video game _____

   sports star _____

   movie star _____

   fast-food restaurant _____

Role and Status

Role and status are sociological terms. *Role* refers to the behavior expected of a person who occupies a particular position in society. For example, there are certain behaviors expected of students, such as attending school regularly, obeying the teacher, and completing assignments. *Status* refers to the position a person occupies in relation to others, as well as the degree of prestige vested in the position. For example, the status of "teacher" is different from that of "student."

The roles of people who would be present at a football game are presented below. List some of the expected behaviors for each role on the spaces provided. Then, based on your personal opinion, rank the status of each role, from highest (1) to lowest (10), by putting the appropriate number on the blank next to the role.

Announcer _____

_____
_____
_____

Assistant Coach _____

_____
_____
_____

Trainer _____

_____
_____
_____

Quarterback _____

_____
_____
_____

Referee _____

_____
_____
_____

Coach _____

_____
_____
_____

Kicker _____

_____
_____
_____

Tackle _____

_____
_____
_____

Ticket Taker _____

_____
_____

Equipment Manager _____

_____
_____

Powerful Influences

List ways groups and institutions influence the event in the center box.

Groups: Institutions:

Clubs

_____

_____

_____

Education

_____

_____

_____

Sports Teams

_____

_____

_____

Politics

_____

_____

_____

Event:
Attending
School Daily.

Family

_____

_____

_____

Economy

_____

_____

_____

Close Friends

_____

_____

_____

Religion

_____

_____

_____

56

Continuity and Change in Society
Teaching Activities

Performance Expectations: Students will identify tensions between individual freedoms or belief systems and group or institutional requirements, describe the role of institutions in furthering continuity and change, and examine how groups and institutions meet personal needs and promote the common good.

Preparation: Make copies of the "Society and Fashion," "Manners Through the Decades," and "Groups and Upward Mobility" student activity sheets.

Society and Fashion (page 58)

One way students express their individuality (and, simultaneously, their peer group conformity) is through their clothing. This activity sheet gives students an opportunity to analyze tensions that often exist between students and adults when it comes to standards of dress. To extend this concept, discuss other areas of tension that exist between individuals and the larger society, such as government health and safety regulations, that infringe on an individual's rights in certain areas.

Manners Through the Decades (page 59)

This activity sheet deals with social expectations and their effect on individual behavior. After students complete the activity, discuss any changes between then and now that were identified. Are people's manners today better, worse, the same, or simply different from the manners of people in the 1950s? What role do manners play in social relationships? Are they necessary? As a follow-up activity, have students interview older adults to see whether they believe manners have changed for the better or worse.

Groups and Upward Mobility (page 60)

This activity sheet will help students identify some groups in American society that have been denied access to political, social, and economic opportunities. Assign students the task of researching the following individuals and social groups that have worked to reform society: the pre-Civil War abolitionists, Samuel Gompers and the labor movement, Cesar Chavez and the United Farm Workers, the peace movement in the 1960s, "Right to Life" organizations, the civil rights movement and Martin Luther King, Jr., environmental groups like the Sierra Club, groups opposed to nuclear power, senior citizens groups like the Gray Panthers, and Betty Friedan and the women's movement.

Name _____

Society and Fashion

Although clothing styles change over time and differ across age groups, one thing seems to remain the same—the tendency of the older generation to criticize the clothes worn by the younger members of society. Do you like the way these two students are dressed? Are they dressed appropriately for school?

I like/do not like what they are wearing because:

_____
_____
_____
_____
_____
_____
_____
_____

I do/do not think they are dressed appropriately for school because:

_____
_____
_____
_____
_____
_____
_____
_____

I do/do not think they would violate my school's dress code because:

_____
_____
_____
_____
_____

Manners Through the Decades

Back in the 1950s, a man tipped his hat when he met a lady, and when he went walking with her, he took the side closest to the street. Every society has its accepted ways of doing things. *Manners* are polite ways of doing things. On the left side of the chart are some manners that were encouraged in the 1950s. On the right side of the page, explain how these manners compare to today's manners in the same situations.

Then	Now
1. Greeting: Always say "Hello, sir" or "Hello, madam" when meeting an adult.	
2. Requesting/receiving: Remember to say "please," "thank you," and "you're welcome."	
3. In public: Never smoke, chew gum, or eat on the street.	
4. On a bus, train, or subway: Never remain seated while an older woman is standing.	
5. Dating: Ladies do not kiss on the first date.	
6. Male manners: Boys carry parcels and open doors for women, stand up when a girl or an adult comes in the room, and help a woman remove her coat.	
7. Talking: Never gossip or interrupt.	
8. The family: Introduce new friends to your family.	
9. Dining out: Boys wear coat and tie when going out on a date to a restaurant. Girls wear skirts below the knee.	

Groups and Upward Mobility

Some ethnic groups in American society suffer more from poverty than others. Poverty is a main obstacle to upward mobility. *Upward mobility* refers to the ability of an individual or group to climb up the economic ladder in our society. Poverty holds people back from getting the training and skills they need to obtain high-paying jobs. The statistical data below shows the median family income for white, African-American, and Hispanic families in 1980 and 1992. (*Median* income is the midpoint that divides all incomes into two groups, upper half and lower half.) Use the data and other information to answer the questions below.

Median Family Income	1980	1992
White families	$21,904	$38,909
African-American families	$12,674	$21,106
Hispanic families	$14,716	$23,901

Source: U.S. Bureau of the Census

1. Which ethnic group had the highest median income in 1992? _____

2. Which ethnic group had the lowest median income in 1992? _____

3. Which ethnic group had the greatest percentage of increase between 1980 and 1992?

    _____

4. What was the dollar difference between a white and an African-American family's median income in 1992? _____

Research the history of African-Americans and Hispanics in the United States. On the blank spaces below, describe some of the past and present obstacles to upward mobility for each group.

African-Americans

_____

_____

_____

_____

Hispanics

_____

_____

_____

_____

Power, Authority, and Governance

CHAPTER 6
Power, Authority, and Governance

Note to the Teacher: Students need to know why and how decisions that affect society are made. They need to be familiar with the philosophies and structures of different types of governments. And, finally, students should know what it means to be a citizen of the his or her country. This unit affords students an opportunity to explore the United States governmental system, examine sources of international cooperation and conflict, and grapple with budgetary choices. Such experiences should help students develop and make informed and reasoned decisions for their own and the public good.

Unit Goal: The purpose of this unit is to help students study how people create and change structures of power, authority, and governance; apply skills in processing information; and express creative abilities.

Materials: This unit includes the following resources: teacher and student bibliographies, activities on power, authority, and governance from multiple content areas, a reproducible student information sheet about the topic, and reproducible student activity sheets for independent study.

RESOURCES
For Teachers:
McClenaghan, William A. *Magruder's American Government.* Newton, MA: Allyn and Bacon, 1985.

Schlesinger, Arthur M., Jr. *The Imperial Presidency.* Boston: Houghton Mifflin, 1973.

For Students:
Bernotas, Bob. *The Federal Government: How It Works.* New York: Chelsea House, 1990.

Lewis, Barbara A. *The Kid's Guide to Social Action.* Minneapolis, MN: Free Spirit Publishing, 1991.

Meltzer, Milton. *American Politics: How It Really Works.* New York: Morrow Junior Books, 1989.

Our Unique Government
Teaching Activities

Performance Expectations: Students will describe the purpose of different forms of government, identify U.S. governmental leaders and describe their duties, identify and describe the basic features of the U.S. political system, and identify how cabinet departments in the federal government attempt to meet the needs and wants of Americans.

Preparation: Make individual copies of the student information sheet "Power, Authority, and Governance," and the "Gallery of Government Leaders," "Checks and Balances," and "Cabinet Departments" student activity sheets.

Introduction

In a nutshell, government is about exercising power to regulate and control people. The information sheet "Power, Authority, and Governance" explains how different types of governments exercise power. To give students a sense of personal empowerment, let them participate in making a set of rules for some upcoming activity. This might include a trip to the library or a classroom game. Then lead them in a discussion about how the rules should be enforced. As students share their ideas about rules, relate their comments to the society at large. Ask: What is the best way for people in a nation to be ruled? After students respond to this question, let them read the information sheet silently.

Gallery of Government Leaders (page 65)

After students have gathered information about the nation's leaders, let them use this material to create a skit in which student volunteers assume the roles of the leaders. The leaders can talk about their respective jobs in Washington, D.C., and the rest of the class can role-play a group of visitors from another country. To add realism, ask the participants in the skit to dress in appropriate attire.

Checks and Balances (page 66)

Learning the significance of *separation of powers* and *checks and balances* is vital for a true understanding of our federal system of government. Once students are familiar with the powers and duties of the three branches of government, you can structure the class as a microcosm of the federal government in which students are assigned to play members of one of the branches. Some of the situations students can simulate include a congressional debate of a treaty, a Supreme Court decision regarding whether or not a law is constitutional, and the president's decision about whether or not to veto a bill.

Cabinet Departments (page 67)

Assign each group of two or three students the task of researching the history and function of one of the cabinet departments. The groups can present their reports orally to the class.

Power, Authority, and Governance

Every society has a *government*, or organized system, to regulate and control its people. The Sumerian civilization developed the world's first system of government in Mesopotamia, or present-day Iraq, over 5,000 years ago. Hammurabi, a Babylonian ruler of Mesopotamia from 1792-1750 B.C., was one of the first people to develop a code of laws.

In all of history there have been many different types of government, and none of them have ever been exactly the same. Three very different and very influential forms of government are described briefly below.

In a *theocracy*, since the right to govern is considered to come directly from the gods, there is no reason to question a ruler's authority. Many of the ancient civilizations, including Sumer, Babylon, and Egypt, were theocracies. In the seventeenth and eighteenth centuries, the idea that God gave kings and queens the right to rule other people was widely accepted in Europe. The Puritans in Massachusetts also established a theocracy.

Over 2,000 years ago, the two powerful Greek city-states of Sparta and Athens fought each other over political control. Sparta was ruled by an *oligarchical* form of government, in which authority to rule rested with only a few privileged people. Every aspect of a Spartan citizen's life—including education, work, marriage, and child rearing—was controlled by the government. The punishment for disobedience in Sparta ranged from whippings to death.

In contrast, Athens had created a new kind of government, called a *democracy*, in which authority to rule rested with all of its citizens. Every Athenian citizen had an equal chance to help make political decisions. Although Sparta won the war against Athens, the idea of democracy has continued. The French Revolution, which began in 1789, led to the spread of democratic ideals throughout Europe. Two hundred years later, the fall of the Berlin Wall in 1989 led to the joining of East and West Germany under democratic leadership and helped make democracy a reality for millions of Europeans.

The torch of democracy has been carried far and wide, but not without difficulty. Americans fought a war with Britain to gain their independence and form a democracy. The U.S. Constitution—including the Bill of Rights and the Fourteenth Amendment—safeguards our democratic form of government and our rights as American citizens. Despite these constitutional guarantees, democratic rights have eluded many Americans, especially non-white ethnic groups and women, throughout our history. Women were not granted the right to vote until 1920, Native Americans were not granted citizenship until 1924, and the segregation of African-Americans into inferior schools was the law of the land until 1954. Although much progress has been made, injustices still exist today, and the struggle to expand democracy's embrace continues. More than 50 years ago, Chief Justice Charles Evans Hughes described the future of our government this way:

> "Democracy will survive only as long as the quick whims of the majority are held in check by the courts in favor of a dominant and lasting sense of justice."

Gallery of Government Leaders

Imagine that you have been asked to tell a group of visitors from another country about your country's national leaders. What would you say about the following leaders? Name the person who currently holds each of the positions. Then explain why each position is important.

	Name of Leader	Why the Leader Is Important
President		
Vice President		
Secretary of State		
Speaker of the House of Representatives		
President Pro Tempore of the Senate		
Chief Justice of the Supreme Court		

Checks and Balances

A unique feature of the U.S. political system is the separation of the powers and duties of the federal government among three branches—legislative, executive, and judicial—so that no one person or group has all of the power. Use classroom and library resources to determine which of the three branches carries out each of the powers and duties listed below. Write the power or duty inside the box under the appropriate branch of government.

Legislative Branch	**Executive Branch**	**Judicial Branch**

Powers and Duties

Signs bills into laws
Decides on meaning of laws
Can pardon people
Can declare war
Commands the armed forces
Appoints judges
Interprets treaties

Can impeach president
Passes laws
Can impeach judges
Enforces laws
Regulates trade
Approves treaties
Appoints ambassadors

Appoints top members of executive branch
Makes treaties with foreign governments
Can propose amendments to the Constitution
Approves appointment of ambassadors
Can declare a law unconstitutional
Can call special sessions of Congress
Approves appointment of judges
Can overturn a president's veto
Can determine the number of justices on the
   Supreme Court

Name _____

Cabinet Departments

The federal government affects your life every day. Listed on the right are the cabinet departments in the executive branch. Listed on the left are some of their major duties. Use library resources to help you correctly match the departments and duties. Write the letters on the blanks in front of the duties. A letter can be used more than once.

Duties

_____ 1. Collects taxes

_____ 2. Enforces government regulations dealing with oil and coal

_____ 3. Helps families buy houses

_____ 4. Distributes financial aid to colleges

_____ 5. Prevents employment discrimination

_____ 6. Operates military bases

_____ 7. Promotes world trade

_____ 8. Enforces federal laws

_____ 9. Operates the national parks

_____10. Helps the president with foreign policy

_____11. Administers social security

_____12. Operates the Federal Aviation Administration (FAA)

_____13. Operates the Food and Drug Administration (FDA)

_____14. Operates the Federal Bureau of Investigation (FBI)

_____15. Conducts the U.S. census

_____16. Inspects and grades food

_____17. Operates the National Weather Service

_____18. Represents the United States at the United Nations

_____19. Operates the Bureau of Indian Affairs

_____20. Operates the national school lunch program

_____21. Provides health care to veterans

Cabinet Departments

A. State
B. Justice
C. Agriculture
D. Transportation
E. Interior
F. Education
G. Health and Human Services
H. Defense
I. Energy
J. Commerce
K. Treasury
L. Housing and Urban Development
M. Labor
N. Veteran Affairs

Making Good Decisions
Teaching Activities

Performance Expectations: Students will examine issues involving individual rights in relation to the general welfare, analyze the obligations of government to its citizens, explain how actions can contribute to conflict and cooperation between and within nations, and analyze the federal budget.

Preparation: Make individual copies of the "Free Speech and the General Welfare," "A Nation's Obligations to Its Citizens," "Conflict and Cooperation," and "Hunger: A World Issue" student activity sheets.

Free Speech and the General Welfare (page 69)

The First Amendment right of free speech is one of America's most important freedoms. Without free speech a democracy could not function. There are times, however, when the government must, for the good of society in general, restrict the speech of individuals or groups. For example, no person has the right to libel or slander another person. As students discuss each of the situations depicted on the activity sheet, make certain they understand why the Constitution guarantees freedom of speech, as well as the other fundamental freedoms of press, assembly, and religion.

A Nation's Obligations to Its Citizens (page 70)

This activity should stimulate discussion about the purpose and role of government. What basic rights should any nation support? Let students investigate particular nations (governments) past and present (such as ancient Greece and Rome, seventeenth- and eighteenth-century France and Britain, Hitler's Germany, Stalin's Soviet Union, and the contemporary governments of Mexico, China, Russia, South Africa, and Iraq, to name a few possibilities) to determine how well they have met their obligations to their citizens.

Conflict and Cooperation (page 71)

During the early 1990s, there was a series of international events that changed (and continue to change) the course of history. Associated with each event are instances of conflict and cooperation. The breakup of the Soviet Union in 1991, for example, brought about unprecedented cooperation between Russia and the United States and the other Western democracies, but it also unleashed violent ethnic conflicts within Russia. Have students work in cooperative groups to complete this activity.

Hunger: A World Issue (page 72)

The social and economic causes of hunger in the less-developed nations of the world are many and complex. The causes include a legacy of colonial exploitation, food production and distribution problems, overdependence on one export for income, overpopulation, lack of a skilled work force, foreign debt, inadequate infrastructure, social injustice, overdependence on the developed world, and corrupt governments. After students complete the activity sheet, discuss whether or not any of these frequently interrelated factors are significant concerns in the nations they investigated.

Free Speech and the General Welfare

The First Amendment gives every person the right to speak freely. But there are limits to free speech. In some cases the government can restrain free speech. What do you think the U.S. Constitution and the courts would say about the following situations?

1. A person falsely shouts "Fire!" in a crowded movie theater.

   _____

   _____

   _____

   _____

2. A musician makes and sells a rock song that promotes killing and other violent acts.

   _____

   _____

   _____

   _____

3. School officials forbid students to wear T-shirts and other clothing that display controversial political messages.

   _____

   _____

   _____

   _____

4. A person makes false and damaging remarks in public about another person.

   _____

   _____

   _____

   _____

A Nation's Obligations to Its Citizens

Imagine that you are a member of a new nation that has just declared its independence. Imagine, too, that you have been selected as a delegate to draft a constitution for the new nation. What should your new nation guarantee its citizens? Below is a list of some possible guarantees or obligations of a nation to its citizens. Which ones would be the most important for your new nation to provide its citizens? Rank the items from "1" for the most important obligation to "12" for the least important obligation. Write the reasons for your ranking on the lines.

Rank   **Reason**

_____ Security _____

_____

_____ Freedom _____

_____

_____ Liberty _____

_____

_____ Order _____

_____

_____ Justice _____

_____

_____ Peace _____

_____

_____ Happiness _____

_____

_____ Equality _____

_____

_____ Education _____

_____

_____ Basic human needs of food, clothing, and shelter _____

_____

_____ Employment opportunities _____

_____

_____ Health care _____

_____

Conflict and Cooperation

Some cataclysmic international and national events that took place in the 1990s are listed below. With your group, use library resources to research the events. Then, on the lines provided, give examples of how each of these events has led to both conflict and cooperation within or among nations.

The breakup of the Soviet Union in 1991.

Examples of conflict:

_____

_____

Examples of cooperation:

_____

_____

The Israeli-Palestinian peace accord signed in 1993.

Examples of conflict:

_____

_____

Examples of cooperation:

_____

_____

The election of South Africa's first black president in 1994.

Examples of conflict:

_____

_____

Examples of cooperation:

_____

_____

The bombing of the federal building in Oklahoma City, Oklahoma, in 1995.

Examples of conflict:

_____

_____

Examples of cooperation:

_____

_____

Hunger: A World Issue

Compared to some places in the world, most people in the United States live a life of relative comfort. Many people who live in the poor, less-developed nations of the world do not have enough food to eat. Most of those countries are located in Central and South America, Asia, and Africa. Choose a less-developed country to investigate. Then gather information about your less-developed nation and the United States on each of the factors italicized in the statements listed below. Finally, for each statement listed, indicate the degree to which you feel the statement applies to your less-developed nation and to the United States. Circle 1 to indicate "very true," 2 to indicate "somewhat true," or 3 to indicate "not at all true." Write the name of your less-developed nation on the line under "Best Describes." After you finish, answer the following questions on a separate sheet of paper: Do you think any of the factors below are linked to the "hunger" issue? When it comes to dealing with world hunger, what role do you think the United States government should play?

	Best Describes _____			Best Describes U.S.A.		
1. There is a high *per capita income*.	3	2	1	3	2	1
2. The nation is at *peace*.	3	2	1	3	2	1
3. The national government is *free of corruption*.	3	2	1	3	2	1
4. The *literacy rate* is high.	3	2	1	3	2	1
5. The nation is plagued by serious or frequent *natural disasters*, such as earthquakes, drought, and so on.	3	2	1	3	2	1
6. *Habitat destruction* and *wildlife extinction* are serious problems.	3	2	1	3	2	1
7. *Individual* and *human rights* are protected.	3	2	1	3	2	1
8. The country is highly *industrialized*.	3	2	1	3	2	1
9. There is plenty of *agricultural land*.	3	2	1	3	2	1
10. *Natural resources* are abundant.	3	2	1	3	2	1

Production,
Distribution, and Consumption

CHAPTER 7
Production, Distribution, and Consumption

Note to the Teacher: Investing in the stock market, being a smart shopper, identifying financial goals, creating a successful business, balancing the family budget, and spending tax dollars wisely are just a few of the fascinating and down-to-earth topics that fall under the domain of economics. Economics is one of the most important subjects that students will need to study and understand. Yet even adults can be mystified by tax codes and personal financial planning, not to mention the complexities of the U.S. and global economies. This unit introduces students to some basic economic concepts and involves them in practical, concrete applications.

Unit Goal: The purpose of this unit is to help students understand the concepts of production, distribution, and consumption, apply skill in gathering and processing information, and express creative abilities.

Materials: This unit includes the following resources: teacher and student bibliographies, teaching activities, a reproducible student information sheet containing concise and interesting facts, and reproducible student activity pages for independent study.

RESOURCES

For Teachers:

Theobald, Robert. *The Rapids of Change: Social Entrepreneurship in Turbulent Times.* Indianapolis, IN: Knowledge Systems, Inc., 1987.

For Students:

Cavin, Ruth. *A Matter of Money: What Do You Do With a Dollar?* New York: Phillips, 1978.

Faber, Doris. *Wall Street: A Story of Fortunes and Finance.* New York: Harper & Row, 1979.

Maybury, Rick. *Whatever Happened to Penny Candy?* Placerville, CA: Bluestocking Press, 1993.

O'Toole, Thomas. *Global Economics.* Minneapolis, MN: Lerner Publications, 1991.

Sattler, Helen Roney. *Dollars From Dandelions: 101 Ways to Earn Money.* New York: Lothrop, Lee & Shephard, 1979.

Scott, Elaine. *Stocks and Bonds, Profits and Losses: A Quick Look at Financial Markets.* New York: Franklin Watts, 1985.

The Economy and You
Teaching Activities

Performance Expectations: Students will describe the concepts of production, distribution, and consumption, examine how values and beliefs influence economic decisions, and develop a plan for achieving a financial goal.

Preparation: Make individual copies of the "Some Economic Essentials" student information sheet and the "Economic Decisions," "Comparison Shopping," and "Long-Range Financial Goals" student activity sheets.

Introduction
To introduce the idea that economics is about choices related to production, distribution, and consumption, hold up a pencil. Ask students to identify the resources that were required to produce it.

- raw materials (wood, chemicals, iron ore, graphite, rubber)
- skilled workers and managers
- capital (money and equipment to make and assemble parts)
- distribution (the transportation systems required to move raw materials to factories and finished pencils to market)
- consumers (the people who buy and use pencils).

This brief study of the economics of pencils should prepare the students for the "Some Economic Essentials" information sheet, which they can read silently.

Economic Decisions (page 77)
After students complete their rankings of the clothing items and have determined their prices, they should be interested in comparing their results with one another. Have them respond to the following questions: Were some students more successful at finding the best buys for the money than others? What factors make a particular clothing item, such as jeans, desirable? To what extent does advertising play a role in the students' economic decisions?

Comparison Shopping (page 78)
This hands-on activity is a great way to introduce students to consumer economics. After students have completed their shopping surveys, assign them to small groups of three or four students and let the groups discuss the following questions: Can consumers save money by doing comparison shopping? Is comparison shopping too time consuming to be a real economic benefit? Are no-name brands a good buy, when compared to their name-brand competition?

Long-Range Financial Goals (page 79)
Now is an excellent time for students to identify a worthwhile goal for saving money. Their foresight today will help make their dreams come true tomorrow. Help them explore local part-time and summer job opportunities, and lead them in a discussion of the importance of saving a portion of their income on a regular basis. Ask a local banker to speak to the class about starting a savings account.

Some Economic Essentials

Make a list of all the things you want, both now and in the future. Does your list include things like a big-screen TV, designer-label clothing, vacations to faraway and exotic places, tickets to music concerts, a flashy car, a waterfront mansion, and other luxuries? One fundamental idea of economics is that people have unlimited wants. Another basic idea of economics is that the resources used to produce goods and services are scarce. Resources such as land, skilled labor, raw materials, and money are always in short supply. *Economics* is the study of how scarce resources are allocated or used. Everyday, people must make choices related to the production, distribution, and consumption of scarce resources.

Choices must be made about the three basic *factors of production*, or resources, used to produce goods and services. *Land*, including natural resources, is an important factor of production. But some land is not used in the production process. Instead, it is protected so that rare animal and plant species will continue to have the habitats they need to survive, or it is kept in its natural condition for people to enjoy. If certain resources are available for use, then decisions must be made regarding how they will be used. Trees, for example, can be used in the production of a multitude of goods, including lumber, plywood, pencils, chopsticks, paper, furniture, railroad ties, and telephone poles, to name a few. *Labor* is another factor of production. In the high-tech workplace of the future, industries will need people who can adapt to new technologies and learn complex procedures. *Capital* is the third factor in the production process. Capital refers to money, buildings, and equipment (including new technology) used to produce and move goods and services.

To be profitable, goods and services must reach the marketplace. This requires an effective *distribution* system. In the 1890s, it took the fastest sailing ship 35 days to carry cargo from San Francisco to Sydney, Australia. Today, jet passenger and cargo planes move people and things around the world in hours. One of the most important products in today's global economy is information. With computers, television, communication satellites, and faxes, information can be transmitted through a global network in seconds. In less time than it takes you to walk to the water fountain, a businessperson in San Francisco can access information from almost anywhere on the planet and transmit it to Sydney. Technological advances are moving products around the world faster, thus increasing productivity.

Like billions of other people worldwide, you are involved in the *consumption*, or the buying and using, of goods and services. Knowing more about economics can help you make better consumer choices. On a personal level, you need to know how to plan a budget, invest your money safely, and save for the future. And you need to understand the national economy so that you can make intelligent decisions about how government can reduce the national debt and spend our tax dollars wisely.

Economic Decisions

Income earned from work is the main source of money for most families. Every family must decide how to spend limited income wisely. Your task is to decide how to spend $300 on new clothes for school. You, of course, will try to choose clothes that satisfy as many of your wants as possible. You also want to get the most value for your money. To help you develop your shopping priorities, rank the clothing items listed below from "1," most wanted item, to "15," least wanted item. You may delete items from the list and/or add other items to the list. Then use catalogs, advertisements, and other sources to track down the best prices for the items. Write the prices on the spaces provided. Can you purchase your wardrobe for $300 or less?

Ranking		**Sale Price**
_____	hat	_____
_____	sweater	_____
_____	two pairs of pants and/or skirts	_____
_____	jeans	_____
_____	button shirt or blouse	_____
_____	six pairs of socks	_____
_____	leather shoes	_____
_____	jacket	_____
_____	belt	_____
_____	coat	_____
_____	six pairs of underwear	_____
_____	gloves	_____
_____	pullover knit shirt or T-shirt	_____
_____	sweatshirt	_____
_____	sports shoes	_____
_____	(write name of item)	_____
_____	(write name of item)	_____
	Total $	_____

Comparison Shopping

In the mid-1990s, a typical monthly food budget for a family with two adults and two school-age children ranged from around $377 to $725. An effective food shopper compares the prices of food items of the same brand at different stores. Use newspaper advertisements and information you can collect from stores to compare the prices of the food items listed below. For each item, compare the prices of a well-known national name brand in two stores as well as the prices of a no-name (store or generic name) brand. For each comparison, make certain the weight, quantity, or volume of food in the containers is the same.

	Name of Store 1 _____		Name of Store 2 _____	
	Prices		**Prices**	
	National	**No-Name**	**National**	**No-Name**
Food Items				
spaghetti (1 lb.)	$_____	$_____	$_____	$_____
corn flakes cereal (12 oz.)	$_____	$_____	$_____	$_____
spaghetti sauce (28 oz.)	$_____	$_____	$_____	$_____
frozen corn (10 oz.)	$_____	$_____	$_____	$_____
frozen orange juice (12 oz.)	$_____	$_____	$_____	$_____
milk (1 gal.)	$_____	$_____	$_____	$_____
American cheese (12 oz.)	$_____	$_____	$_____	$_____
pork and beans (16 oz.)	$_____	$_____	$_____	$_____
ketchup (14 oz.)	$_____	$_____	$_____	$_____
cola soft drink (2 liter)	$_____	$_____	$_____	$_____
sugar (5 lbs.)	$_____	$_____	$_____	$_____
flour (5 lbs.)	$_____	$_____	$_____	$_____
frozen pizza (24 oz.)	$_____	$_____	$_____	$_____
hot dogs (12 oz.)	$_____	$_____	$_____	$_____
bread (1 loaf)	$_____	$_____	$_____	$_____
potato chips (7 oz.)	$_____	$_____	$_____	$_____
frozen fish sticks (48 oz.)	$_____	$_____	$_____	$_____
frozen French fries	$_____	$_____	$_____	$_____
frozen waffles (pkg. of 8)	$_____	$_____	$_____	$_____
pancake mix (32 oz.)	$_____	$_____	$_____	$_____
pancake syrup (12 oz.)	$_____	$_____	$_____	$_____
green beans (14.5 oz.)	$_____	$_____	$_____	$_____
Totals	$_____	$_____	$_____	$_____

Long-Range Financial Goals

Choose an important long-range financial goal for yourself. "Long-range goal," in this case, means a goal that you would like to obtain within 10 years from now. The goal might be to save enough money to buy a new car, take a vacation to Europe, or pay for the first year of college, to name a few possibilities. After you have picked a goal and determined the amount of money needed, describe the steps you will have to take to achieve your goal. Use the chart below to describe each of the steps.

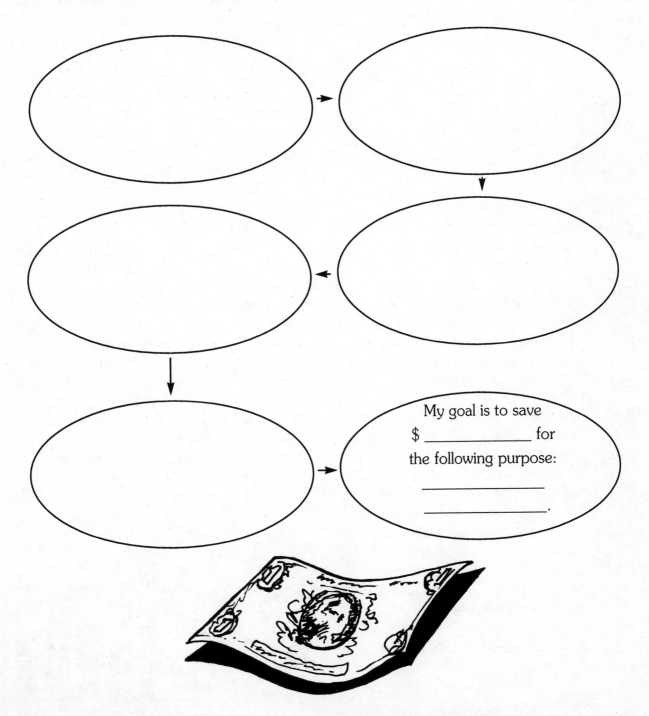

My goal is to save
$ _____ for
the following purpose:
_____
_____.

The Economy in Action

Teaching Activities

Performance Expectations: Students will identify examples of the components of an economic system, describe the influence of important American entrepreneurs on the U.S. economy, study the performance of selected stocks, and analyze the federal budget.

Preparation: Make individual copies of the "Exploring Our Economic System," "America's Rich and Famous Entrepreneurs," "Pick Five," and "Decisions! Decisions! Decisions!" student activity sheets.

Exploring Our Economic System (page 81)

After students track down the names of individuals and organizations that are part of the local/regional economic system, they might want to interview a business entrepreneur, manager, government agency employee, or union leader to find out more about the person's job and how it relates to the economy as a whole.

America's Rich and Famous Entrepreneurs (page 82)

Once students learn about the five famous entrepreneurs highlighted on the activity sheet, they should be ready to speculate about entrepreneurship in the twenty-first century. What will those future times be like? What kinds of discoveries will be made? What new technologies will be invented? How will the world be changed? Have students create future scenarios that describe entrepreneurs operating in areas like ecology, health, education, and industry.

Pick Five (page 83)

To make this activity even more realistic, you may want to give small groups of three or four students a set amount of money, say $10,000, to invest in the market. Students can pick their five stocks and then use their math skills to figure out how many shares they can afford to "buy" with the money. (Stocks are usually purchased in multiples of 100 shares.) At the end of three weeks, they can "sell" their five stocks at the closing prices and calculate their profit or loss. Have students make a graph to display each stock's performance.

Decisions! Decisions! Decisions! (page 84)

An issue always in the news is the federal budget. The size of the total budget and various federal outlays reflect the government's priorities. Bigger budgets usually mean more taxes and/or borrowing (income) to cover the costs of programs (outlays). This activity gives students an opportunity to analyze a recent budget and decide their own priorities for government. Students can investigate the various categories of government programs, such as national defense, to determine the services they provide citizens.

Exploring Our Economic System

Economic systems within nations determine how scarce resources are used. Some important elements of our economic system are listed below. Use information gathered from the media and your own experience to identify five specific examples of each of the elements. Write the examples on the lines provided below.

Managers (These are people who operate businesses. They may or may not own them. Write the names and businesses below.)

1. _____
2. _____
3. _____
4. _____
5. _____

Government Agencies (List the names of agencies that regulate businesses, corporations, banks, imports and exports, or the money system.)

1. _____
2. _____
3. _____
4. _____
5. _____

Workers (These are people who are employed to produce goods and services. Write the names and places of employment below.)

1. _____
2. _____
3. _____
4. _____
5. _____

Consumers (These are people who buy goods and services. Write the names of five consumers and list a recent purchase for each one.)

1. _____
2. _____
3. _____
4. _____
5. _____

Banks (List the names below.)

1. _____
2. _____
3. _____
4. _____
5. _____

Labor Unions (List the names below.)

1. _____
2. _____
3. _____
4. _____
5. _____

Entrepreneurs (These are people who create and run new businesses. Write the names and businesses below.)

1. _____
2. _____
3. _____
4. _____
5. _____

Businesses and/or Corporations (Write the names of local or regional companies below.)

1. _____
2. _____
3. _____
4. _____
5. _____

America's Rich and Famous Entrepreneurs

Entrepreneurs are people who create and run businesses and industries. Listed below are five of America's richest and most famous entrepreneurs. Your task is to use library resources to find out about their lives. What were their business accomplishments? How did each of these individuals achieve business success? Write your answers to these questions on the lines provided.

Andrew Carnegie

_____
_____
_____
_____

Thomas Edison

_____
_____
_____
_____

John D. Rockefeller

_____
_____
_____
_____

J. Pierpont Morgan

_____
_____
_____
_____

Bill Gates

_____
_____
_____
_____

Pick Five

Many of the most important businesses and industries in the world are corporations. *Corporations* are owned by individuals who have purchased shares of stock in the companies. A person who owns one or more shares of stock in a corporation is called a *stockholder*. Some large corporations, such as American Telephone & Telegraph, have millions of stockholders. Shares of stock are bought and sold Monday through Friday on the New York Stock Exchange (NYSE) and other major exchanges around the world. Investing money in the stock market is risky. The price of a share of stock can go up, but it can also go down in value. Investors want to buy stocks at a low price and sell them at a high price, but sometimes just the opposite happens. During the Great Depression of the 1930s, some stocks worth hundreds of dollars a share dropped quickly to a few dollars a share. As a result, some corporations were forced to shut down and many stockholders lost all of the money they had invested.

The daily stock prices are listed in the business section of many newspapers. Your task is to select five stocks from the daily list and follow their performance for three weeks. Corporations are listed by their abbreviations in the newspapers. For example, American Telephone & Telegraph is AT&T, Coca-Cola is CocaCl, and McDonald's is McDnlds. Write the abbreviations for your stocks in the blank spaces. Then consult your local newspaper daily and write each day's closing price on the chart below. What happens to your stocks? Do they go up or down?

Stock #1

Week 1					Week 2					Week 3				
M	T	W	Th	F	M	T	W	Th	F	M	T	W	Th	F

_____

Stock #2

Week 1					Week 2					Week 3				
M	T	W	Th	F	M	T	W	Th	F	M	T	W	Th	F

_____

Stock #3

Week 1					Week 2					Week 3				
M	T	W	Th	F	M	T	W	Th	F	M	T	W	Th	F

_____

Stock #4

Week 1					Week 2					Week 3				
M	T	W	Th	F	M	T	W	Th	F	M	T	W	Th	F

_____

Stock#5

Week 1					Week 2					Week 3				
M	T	W	Th	F	M	T	W	Th	F	M	T	W	Th	F

_____

Decisions! Decisions! Decisions!

On or before the first Monday in February of each year, the President is required by law to submit to the Congress the federal government's budget proposal for the fiscal (or financial) year that begins the following October. In a recent fiscal year, the federal government's income was $1,154 billion and outlays (or expenses) were $1,408 billion, leaving a deficit (or loss) of $254 billion. Below are pie charts that show the relative sizes of the major categories of federal income and outlays for that year. Use the charts to answer the questions below.

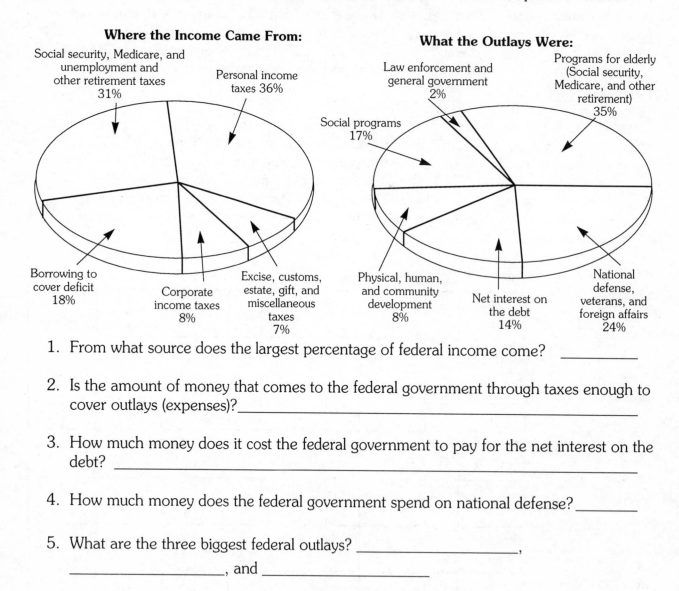

Where the Income Came From:

Social security, Medicare, and unemployment and other retirement taxes 31%

Personal income taxes 36%

Borrowing to cover deficit 18%

Corporate income taxes 8%

Excise, customs, estate, gift, and miscellaneous taxes 7%

What the Outlays Were:

Law enforcement and general government 2%

Programs for elderly (Social security, Medicare, and other retirement) 35%

Social programs 17%

Physical, human, and community development 8%

Net interest on the debt 14%

National defense, veterans, and foreign affairs 24%

1. From what source does the largest percentage of federal income come? _____

2. Is the amount of money that comes to the federal government through taxes enough to cover outlays (expenses)?_____

3. How much money does it cost the federal government to pay for the net interest on the debt? _____

4. How much money does the federal government spend on national defense?_____

5. What are the three biggest federal outlays? _____,
   _____, and _____

6. If you were in charge of the federal budget, how would you slice the money pie for outlays? On a separate sheet of paper, draw a pie chart that shows how you would spend the money. For each of the categories on the outlays pie chart, decide what percentage of money in the budget it should receive. (Remember that the sum of the percentages must equal 100.)

Science,
Technology, and Society

FS-10187 Teaching the Ten Themes of Social Studies

CHAPTER 8
Science, Technology, and Society

Note to the Teacher: The fundamental purpose of schooling has always been knowledge acquisition. But the basic tools of learning are changing radically. Today's students are relying less on the old tools of paper, pencils, and books, and more on advanced technologies, such as computers, the Internet, and CD-ROMs, to access information instantly. Nowadays, classroom computers are plugged into an international communications network that puts the whole world at students' fingertips. Faster and smarter machines also are changing homes, communities, and the workplace. Because of these ongoing revolutionary changes in the way people live and work, the need to understand how science, technology, and society interact has never been greater than now.

Unit Goal: The purpose of this unit is to help students explore the relationships among science, technology, and society, apply skill in gathering and processing information, and express creative abilities.

Materials: This unit contains the following resources: student and teacher bibliographies, teaching activities, a reproducible student information sheet containing facts on science, technology and society, and reproducible student activity sheets for independent study.

RESOURCES
For Teachers:
Gunton, Tony. *The Penguin Dictionary of Information Technology and Computer Science*. New York: Penguin Books, 1992.

For Students:
Evans, Peter. *Technology 2000*. New York: Facts on File, 1985.

Martin, Paul D. *Science: It's Changing Your World*. Washington, D.C.: National Geographic Society, 1985.

McKie, Robin. *Technology*. New York: Franklin Watts, 1984.

Skurzynski, Gloria. *Get the Message: Telecommunications in Your High-Tech World*. New York: Bradbury Press, 1993.

Spencer, Jean W. *Careers Inside the World of Technology*. New York: Rosen Publishing Group, 1995.

The Science-Society Connection
Teaching Activities

Performance Expectations: Students will examine how science and technology have changed people's perceptions of the social and natural world, express their creative abilities designing a robot, and survey their everyday involvement with technology.

Preparation: Make individual copies of the "Technology and You" student information sheet and the "Technology: What Do You Think?" "Robot Design," and "Technology Checklist" student activity sheets.

Introduction
To get students thinking about the science-society connection, ask them to provide recent examples of science and technology's impact on society, such as genetic engineering, new medicines, or new safety features on cars. After students read the "Technology and You" information sheet, discuss the gnat robot concept. Do students believe science and technology can progress to a level that would make such microscopic devices feasible?

Technology: What Do You Think? (page 89)
Many experts have discussed the societal implications of the development of increasingly faster and smarter machines. After students finish the activity sheet, let them share their answers with a classmate. Remind students that technology includes ideas as well as tools and machines. Ask students to debate the following assertion: To survive, society must invent new ideas to help people cope with rapid social change.

Robot Design (page 90)
Designing robots will give students an opportunity to demonstrate their creative abilities. To get them started, provide pictures of various types of animals. Encourage them to "borrow" body parts from different animals. As an extension activity, let students make three-dimensional models of their robots and display them in the classroom.

Technology Checklist (page 91)
This activity should make students more aware of the importance and pervasiveness of technology in their everyday lives. Students should be able to cite multiple examples of technology that they use. If some students are frequent users of more specialized technologies, such as musical instruments or sports equipment, let them describe the devices to the class.

Technology Survey
Have students use the list of technological devices found in "Technology Checklist" to survey elderly people to determine whether or not any of the items were used by them when they were teenagers. This activity should highlight the fact that some technologies were not available until fairly recently.

Technology and You

Someday you may own a bunch of mobile robots the size of gnats and covered with microsensors that can see, smell, and feel. You could use them to make you a sandwich, wash your car, or check the dog for fleas. The potential societal applications for such a tiny device are fascinating to speculate about. One microrobot could crawl into an underground electrical conduit to fix a broken wire. Others could fly over fields to check if crops needed water, hover over homes to protect against intruders, or maneuver around a space station to inspect its outer surface for microscopic cracks. Millions could swim along the side of a ship and scrub away at the barnacles. Does this sound too far-fetched? Not according to research scientist Anita Flynn, who describes these possibilities for this insect-like robot in an article that focuses on artificial intelligence technology. Although such robots have not been invented yet, she believes that someday they might be as cheap, disposable, and commonplace as ballpoint pens.

Science is a journey into the unknown. Scientists generate knowledge about the world. They are discoverers. Technology is dependent on science. Scientific breakthroughs in physics, for example, have led to the development of transistors and chips, two technological advances that have transformed society. Before the arrival of those technologies, computers used thousands of vacuum tubes, covered an area the size of a house, and performed thousands of operations per second. In comparison, today's desktop computers, some with one million transistors contained within a single microchip, are capable of millions of operations per second! So, if the pattern of making smaller and smarter computers continues, just remember in the future to take a close look at that gnat buzzing near your ear. You never know, it just might be a robot!

Advances in computer technology have brought revolutionary changes to society. Today, governments, businesses, research centers, schools, and homes are interconnected by a computer network that lets people access information and one another anytime and anyplace. In today's high-tech schools, many students are using computers to draft and edit papers, design robots, practice foreign languages, study human anatomy, send and receive E-mail, access the Internet and CD-ROMs for research, and perform and display science experiments, to cite just a few examples.

Modern technology has made our lives better in many ways. But technology also can have negative spin-offs. For example, today's cash registers, with their built-in computers that make change, allow some businesses to hire clerks who do not know simple arithmetic, thereby making it appear that basic math skills are unimportant in the workplace. That sends the wrong message to students. In fact, just the opposite is true. The better, higher-paying high-tech jobs of the future will require *more* education, not less.

Technology: What Do You Think?

Three statements about technology are stated below. On the lines below each statement, tell if you think the statement is accurate and if it describes real conditions as you know them. Be certain to explain your reasons and cite evidence to support your thinking.

1. Technology is increasing the pace of work.

   _____
   _____
   _____
   _____
   _____
   _____

2. Technology is making work more specialized.

   _____
   _____
   _____
   _____
   _____
   _____

3. Technology is becoming smarter.

   _____
   _____
   _____
   _____
   _____

Robot Design

Creating a new, real animal that looked like this would be impossible. But new machines that can do real work are being invented all the time. Using the anatomy of one or more animals as your inspiration, draw a design for a robot that can perform a specific task in the home, school, or workplace. Be creative and try to include all the "bells and whistles" that will make your design unique. Draw your robot in the space below.

Technology Checklist

Listed below are a variety of familiar technological devices found at home and in school. Place a check in the box beside each device you have used during the past 24 hours.

☐ Toaster	☐ Stereo system
☐ Refrigerator	☐ Ballpoint pen
☐ Computer	☐ Water fountain
☐ Television	☐ Soft drink dispenser
☐ Pencil sharpener	☐ Snack food dispenser
☐ Radio	☐ Air conditioner/Furnace
☐ VCR	☐ Fan
☐ Light bulb	☐ Fax
☐ Camcorder	☐ Stapler
☐ Washer/Dryer	☐ Tape dispenser
☐ Camera	☐ Printer
☐ CD player	☐ Car
☐ Personal tape player with headphones	☐ Bus
☐ Microwave oven	☐ Ice dispenser
☐ Telephone	☐ Microscope
☐ Sewing machine	☐ Telescope
☐ Vacuum cleaner	☐ Mountain bike
☐ Electric/Gas range	☐ Leaf blower
☐ Dishwasher	☐ Lawn mower
☐ Calculator	
☐ Iron	
☐ Electric toothbrush	
☐ Watch	
☐ Hair dryer	
☐ Video game player	
☐ Electric can opener	

Machines and People

Teaching Activities

Performance Expectations: Students will examine the influence of technological advancements on various aspects of society, explain the need for laws to govern scientific applications, and analyze issues that arise when technological advancements and societal values conflict.

Preparation: Make individual copies of the "Technology's Impact on People," "Technology Top 20," "The Computer," and "America's Nuclear Power Plants: Let's…" student activity sheets.

Technology's Impact on People (page 93)

Perhaps no invention has affected the course of American history more than the cotton gin. As stated on the student sheet, the device revitalized the institution of slavery in the South, which, in turn, contributed to the sectionalism that eventually divided the nation. To increase motivation, ask volunteers to assume the roles of historical characters. They can present their reports orally to the class clad in homemade costumes that reflect the historical period.

Technology Top 20 (page 94)

First, let students individually rank the 20 items on the list. After they have finished, assign the students to small groups and ask the groups to rank the items. Encourage each group to try to reach a consensus on the rankings. Are there any items on the list that are more essential than others? Make certain that students look for possible interrelationships between items on the list. For example, if the wheel had never been invented, would it have been possible to invent the car?

The Computer (page 95)

Many inventions have disappeared from the scene because the public showed no interest in them. This has not been the case with the computer, however. In a relatively short period of time, the computer has changed almost every aspect of society. It has altered the way people do business, changed communications patterns, and affected people's lifestyles. Ask students to discuss the computer's impact on their own lives. Does the computer help them work faster and better? Do some students prefer not to use computers? Let students gather ads and articles from magazines that describe how computers have changed various aspects of society.

America's Nuclear Power Plants: Let's… (page 96)

Technology gives humans the capability to change the environment in massive ways—sometimes for the better, sometimes for the worse. Encourage students to debate the pros and cons related to the use of nuclear energy to generate electricity in the United States. If possible, have guest speakers with opposing viewpoints on the issue (such as environmental activists and utility industry spokespersons) address the class. Ask students to consider how technology might be used to solve environmental problems, rather than create them.

Technology's Impact on People

The cotton gin had a tremendous impact on the United States. Read the information below about the cotton gin. Use library sources to learn more about the beginning stages of American industrialization. Then imagine how the following nineteenth-century people might have been affected by the invention of the cotton gin: a slave trader, an English textile mill owner, a southern cotton grower, a New England sea merchant, and a southern slave. On a separate sheet of paper, write an essay to describe how these people might have been affected.

The Cotton Gin

The cotton gin, which was patented in 1794, was invented by Eli Whitney. Whitney's invention was unique, but it was prompted by great changes that had taken place and were still taking place thousands of miles away—in England.

The Industrial Revolution started in the middle of the eighteenth century in England with the appearance of machinery to make cotton and wool textiles that were cheaper than handmade cloth. Before long, the Industrial Revolution had spread to the United States, and Americans were using some of the English machines and inventing their own. Because of the big demand for their textiles, the English industries wanted to buy more cotton from the United States. American producers, however, could not supply them with enough, no matter how hard they tried. The problem was cotton seeds. The cotton fibers had to be separated from the seed by hand, slowly and with much difficulty. That is when a renowned Yankee inventor, Eli Whitney, entered the picture. On a visit to Georgia, Whitney learned of the tremendous need for a machine that could do this time-consuming work faster. He immediately put his mind to the task of inventing such a machine. Whitney's newfangled device could do the work of 50 people. With the widespread adoption of the cotton gin, the production of cotton in the South skyrocketed and shipments of the fiber to English textile mills increased greatly.

The consequences of Whitney's invention are just as significant as the reasons for its invention. The introduction of steam-powered cotton gins made the production of cotton even more profitable. Cotton became the chief cash crop in the South. Before the invention of the cotton gin, the institution of slavery was on the decline in the South. But along with the cotton gin and the cotton boom came the need for more and more slaves to work the fields. The revival of slavery in the South and the fear of its spread to other parts of the nation were major causes of the Civil War, which began in 1861.

Technology Top 20

Below are 20 of the major inventions or discoveries in the history of technology. One way to judge the importance of any particular technological advance is to examine its impact on people and the environment. Did the invention or discovery have a ripple effect on society? That is, did it change the way of life of people across groups/societies and through time? Rank the 20 inventions or discoveries listed below from "1" for the most impact on society to "20" for the least impact on society. Be prepared to cite the reasons for your rankings.

_____ the wheel

_____ paper

_____ agriculture

_____ control of fire

_____ stone tools

_____ steam engine

_____ compass

_____ writing system

_____ pottery

_____ airplane

_____ electricity

_____ printing press

_____ photography

_____ penicillin

_____ jet engine

_____ plastic

_____ nuclear reactor

_____ computer

_____ radio

_____ car

Name _____

The Computer

The computer has affected almost every American in one way or another. In the spaces provided, explain how the computer has influenced the various aspects of society highlighted below.

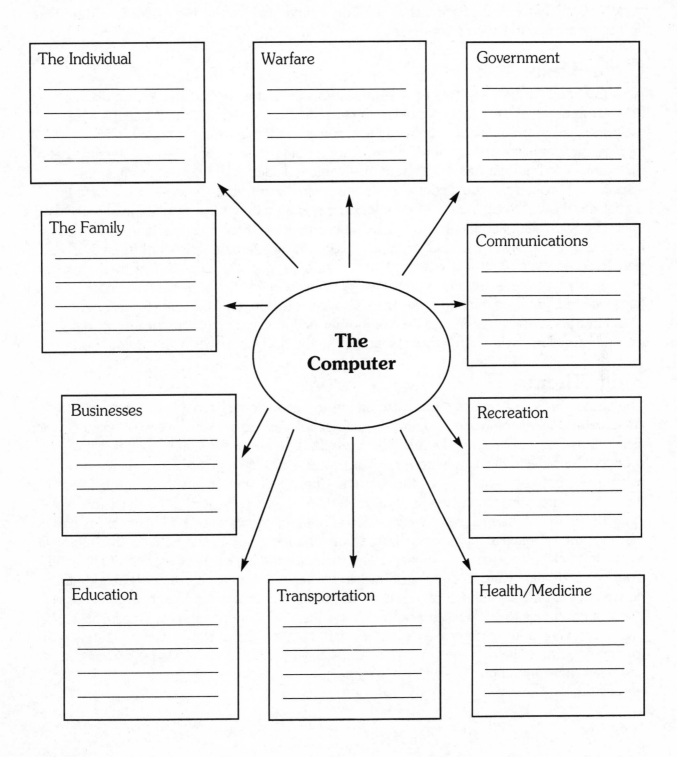

Name _____

America's Nuclear Power Plants: Let's . . .

Read the opposing "editorials" printed below. Then consult library and other sources to develop a personal position on the use of nuclear power in the United States. All things considered, do you think the impact of nuclear energy technology on our society has been good or bad? Write your position statement on a separate sheet of paper. Make certain that you cite evidence to support your position.

Close Them

America's nuclear power plants pose some serious problems for society. As the nuclear reactors in these power plants get older, they become more radioactive. Since the aging reactors need more frequent maintenance, workers at the plants could be exposed to increasingly dangerous doses of radiation. Another big problem, of course, is the disposal of the plants' used nuclear fuel, which remains highly radioactive. If nuclear waste is not disposed of properly, it could contaminate the environment, thereby making it unsafe for humans and other living things. Mechanical and human failure have resulted in serious nuclear power plant accidents, like those that occurred at Three Mile Island in 1979 near Harrisburg, Pennsylvania, and Chernobyl in 1986 in the Ukraine. For all of these reasons, people do not want a nuclear power plant or waste disposal site located near them. Instead of nuclear power, let's use other, safer energy sources—petroleum, natural gas, coal, hydroelectric, geothermal, and solar. Let's also learn to conserve more energy. America's consumption of energy is greater than any other nation's. Let's tighten our energy belt, expand our use of safe energy sources, and close the nuclear power plants down, now!

Keep Them

The United States generates more electricity from nuclear energy than any other country. America also leads the world in operable nuclear power reactors with over 100 (almost twice as many as France, which ranks second). About 22 percent of the United States' total production of electricity comes from nuclear power. Properly regulated and maintained, nuclear power is safe, clean, and efficient. The Chernobyl nuclear power plant explosion was the result of gross mismanagement. Given the openness of our society, the news media's watchdog role, and the federal government's regulatory power over the U.S. nuclear energy industry, the probability that such a disaster could happen here is almost zero. Technology is available to clean up aging power plants and minimize the exposure of workers to radiation. There also are safe ways to dispose of nuclear waste so that no one will be harmed, either now or in the future. America cannot meet its current and projected total energy needs unless it continues to use nuclear power, along with other energy sources. Finally, for military and national security reasons, we cannot allow the United States to be overly dependent on foreign governments for its energy needs. Let's clean up those aging nuclear power plants and keep them running!

Global
Connections

97

CHAPTER 9
Global Connections

Note to the Teacher: America's ability to function successfully in today's interconnected world will depend on the international understandings and attitudes of its citizens. Negative attitudes on the part of students about other cultures and nations are often the result of inadequate and inaccurate information. This unit helps students examine the pattern of relationships between themselves and other peoples and cultures. Students are encouraged to explore issues related to diversity, stereotyping, and global responsibilities.

Unit Goal: The purpose of this unit is to help students explore global connections and interdependence, apply skill in gathering and processing information, and express creative abilities.

Materials: This unit includes the following resources: teacher and student bibliographies, teaching activities, a reproducible student information sheet containing facts on global connections, and reproducible student activity sheets for independent study.

RESOURCES

For Teachers:

Hamilton, John M. *Entangling Alliances: How the Third World Shapes Our Lives*. Cabin John, MD: Seven Locks, 1990.

Hamilton, John M. *Main Street America and the Third World*. Cabin John, MD: Seven Locks, 1986.

For Students:
Books

O'Toole, Thomas. *Global Economics*. Minneapolis: Lerner Publications, 1991.

Pedersen, Anne. *The Kids' Environment Book*. Santa Fe, NM: John Muir Publications, 1991.

Pringle, Laurence. *Our Hungry Earth: The World Food Crisis*. New York: Macmillan, 1976.

Woog, Adam. *The United Nations*. San Diego: Lucent Books, 1994.

Software

Race to Save the Planet. Scholastic Software, Inc., 2931 East McCarty Street, Jefferson City, MO 65101 (800) 541-5513

Being Worldly Wise
Teaching Activities

Performance Expectations: Students will explore how music and other cultural elements can facilitate global understanding, analyze international news stories for examples of conflict, cooperation and interdependence, and describe the effects of technology on global consumerism.

Preparation: Make individual copies of the student information sheet "Examples of Global Connections" and the "Where in the World Has the News Been?" "The World and You," and "Global Rhythms" student activity sheets.

Introduction

To get students thinking globally, hold up a chocolate bar and ask them what it is made of. Point out that chocolate is made from cacao, which is a plant that originated in Latin America and is now grown by many African countries. Make a list on the chalkboard of foods students like that come from other countries. Ask students to think about other ways they are connected to people and nations around the world. Let them silently read the "Examples of Global Connections" student information sheet. According to students' opinions, is increasing globalization a positive or negative trend?

Where in the World Has the News Been? (page 101)

After students have completed this activity, help them analyze each news story to determine if the news event is an example of conflict, cooperation, or interdependence among groups, societies, or nations. What does their analysis tell the class about current world conditions? Can they draw any tentative conclusions?

The World and You (page 102)

Never in history have Americans carried around on their backs and in their packs more international items than today. That message ought to become clear to most students after they draw themselves and label their foreign-made possessions. To extend this activity, ask students to inventory international items found in their homes. Are there some foreign-made items that students would hate to do without? What are they and why would students hate to do without them?

Global Rhythms (page 103)

Challenge students to track down the origin of the types of music and the dances listed on the activity sheet. The next step, of course, is to bring the music itself into the classroom for students to sample and enjoy. Encourage students to bring examples of international music from home. Your school's music teacher and librarian might have world music on tapes and CDs, as well as dances on videotapes. World music suitable for adults and children, including African songs by Ladysmith Black Mambazo and reggae songs from the Caribbean, is available in most community libraries and music stores. There also may be talented students or adults in the community who would be willing to teach traditional songs and dances. In cooperation with other teachers, you might want to plan an all-day international music festival, where world music, dances, and other cultural elements could be showcased.

Examples of Global Connections

What do New York, London, Bonn, Tokyo, Rome, Toronto, Buenos Aires, Johannesburg, Seoul, Sydney, and dozens of other major cities around the world have in common? For one thing, they are all part of the global economy. Because of faster and better transportation and communications systems, banking and manufacturing centers worldwide are becoming more closely linked. Today, most big businesses, like IBM, Nestle, Sony, and BMW, are called multinational corporations because they operate in several countries. Since businesses are always trying to find new markets for their products, the global economy should continue to expand. The globalization of the economy has influenced countries and cultures everywhere. This is especially apparent in the popular culture of the younger generation. Because of the global fashion and entertainment industries' influence, young people around the world are becoming more alike; they often wear the same styles or brands of clothing, watch the same movies and TV shows, and listen to the same music.

People everywhere also are part of one huge interacting, life-sustaining system—Earth's environment. On April 22, 1970, the first Earth Day was celebrated. On that historic day, millions of Americans turned out to protest global pollution and pledge support for actions to protect the environment. Since then, much has been done to save the Earth from destruction. Thoughtful people have worked to preserve natural areas, create green spaces in cities and along roads, clean rivers and lakes, conserve natural resources, reduce air pollution, and recycle waste. But there is still much left to do. Protecting the planet for future generations will require global cooperation and innovative approaches. Fortunately, new technologies are continuously being developed that make it possible for people and nations to work together in new ways. For example, interconnected computers are being used to compile and disseminate up-to-date information about the location and condition of thousands of types of plants, animals, and habitats around the world.

Slowly but surely, people are beginning to realize that putting their heads together is better than bumping them together. For decades, the Earth's two major space powers, the United States and the Soviet Union, operated separate programs, kept their technologies secret, and competed with each other. With the collapse of the Soviet Union in 1991, a new era of international cooperation in space was launched. Now, competition and secrecy are beginning to be replaced by mutual respect and a shared vision. An example of this development occurred in 1995 when astronaut Norman Thagard became the first American to board Russia's *Mir* space station, where he joined Russian cosmonauts for a 115-day stay. Early in the twenty-first century, a permanent, international space station might be orbiting the Earth, manned by six to eight crew members from the United States, Russia, Canada, Britain, France, Japan, and other nations of the world.

Perhaps these and other global connections will begin to free humans of the old limitations that kept them apart—and prevented them from fulfilling their potential.

Where in the World Has the News Been?

Every day, news stories involving various countries around the world appear in the media (newspapers, magazines, radio, and television). Your task is to follow the international news carefully for one week. Make a list of all the countries mentioned in the news for that week. Then locate and label these nations on the map below. On a separate sheet of paper, explain how one of these news stories affects the United States.

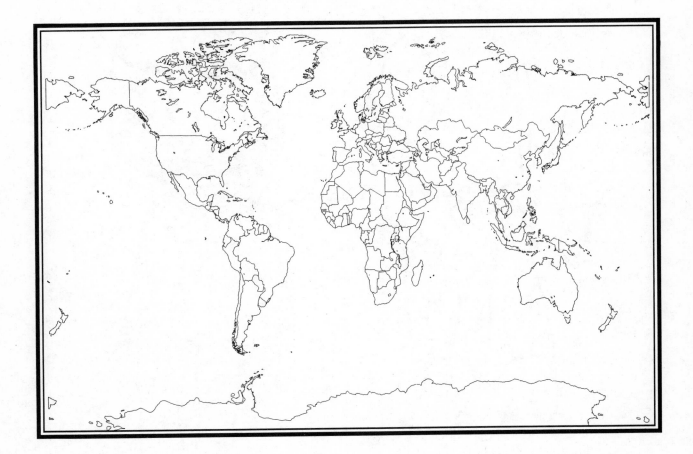

The World and You

The students below are well-connected internationally. On a separate sheet of paper, draw a picture of yourself, and then label all of the foreign-made items that might be found on you during a typical day.

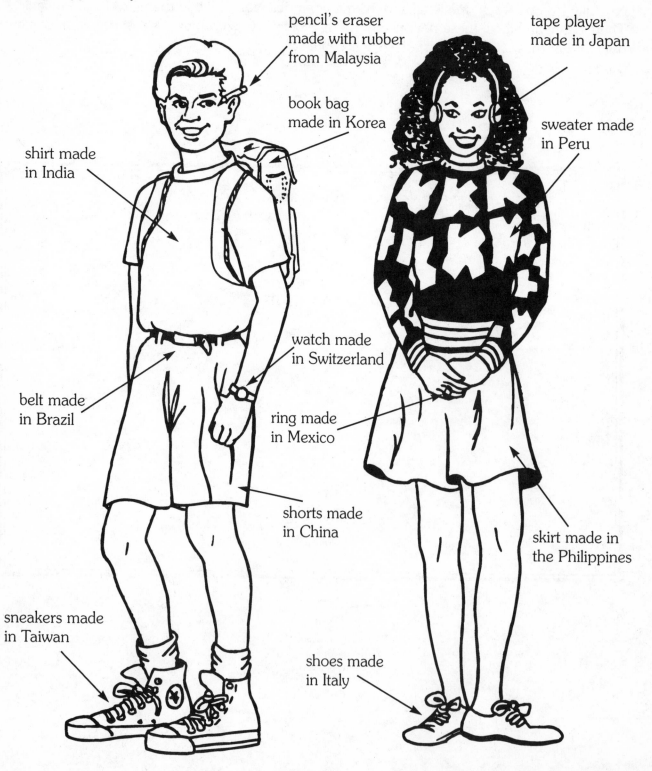

pencil's eraser made with rubber from Malaysia

tape player made in Japan

book bag made in Korea

sweater made in Peru

shirt made in India

watch made in Switzerland

belt made in Brazil

ring made in Mexico

shorts made in China

skirt made in the Philippines

sneakers made in Taiwan

shoes made in Italy

ᴐal Rhythms

One way to make global connections is through music and dance. On the left are listed various countries or areas of the world. On the right are listed some of their traditional dances and music. Use reference materials to match each dance or musical style to its place. See how many you can match!

Places	**Dances and Musical Styles**
_____ 1. Brazil	A. hula
_____ 2. Japan	B. waltz
_____ 3. Mexico	C. flamenco
_____ 4. Zambia	D. makishi
_____ 5. India	E. barong
_____ 6. Spain	F. opera
_____ 7. Middle East	G. polka
_____ 8. England	H. ballet
_____ 9. Russia	I. Maypole dance
_____ 10. Scotland	J. dabkah
_____ 11. Italy	K. hat dance
_____ 12. Jamaica	L. samba
_____ 13. Germany	M. kabuki
_____ 14. Indonesia	N. highland fling
_____ 15. Cuba	O. bharata natyam
_____ 16. Austria	P. schuhplatteltanz
_____ 17. Hawaii	Q. rumba
_____ 18. Bohemia	R. Cossack dance
_____ 19. France	S. czardas
_____ 20. Hungary	T. reggae

Global Interconnections
Teaching Activities

Performance Expectations: Students will analyze global issues, explore global and local connections, and identify and describe the roles of international organizations.

Preparation: Make individual copies of the "Local Connections," "World Traveler," "What on Earth Do They Do?" and "New Symbol" student activity sheets.

Local Connections (page 105)

Young people are frequently unaware of how the outside world affects them personally. People in the community would be good sources of information about the effects of global issues on the community. Encourage students to interview local religious leaders, military leaders, representatives of community and international service organizations, government officials, news reporters, businesspeople, and others who might be knowledgeable of international-local connections.

World Traveler (page 106)

All humans seem to have learned to engage in ethnocentric thinking, which is the tendency to view one's own society and culture as "better" or "superior" to other societies and cultures. In addition, most young Americans have had little or no firsthand experience living in another culture. For these reasons, your students probably have acquired their share of negative stereotypes and misunderstandings about other countries, cultures, and regions of the world. This

activity will give students an opportunity to explore cultural misconceptions and analyze ethnocentric tendencies. Probe to determine whether students have accurate information about the regions they have researched. Discuss the relationship between the seven geographic regions and various global issues.

What on Earth Do They Do? (page 107)

Assign small groups of three or four students the task of explaining and demonstrating the role of one of the international organizations listed on the activity sheet. For example, if students in one group were assigned the Organization of Petroleum Exporting Countries (OPEC), each student could first describe some aspect of OPEC's purpose and functions, and then the group could create a brief skit of an OPEC meeting, in which member nations were arguing about whether or not they should increase or decrease oil production.

New Symbol (page 108)

Because of the growing global economy, there is a strong possibility that many of your students will work for a multinational corporation someday. This activity gives students an opportunity to imagine themselves in such a situation. Have students discuss various global career prospects. Let them discuss the possible educational requirements for international occupations. After students have drawn their company logos, display them on the classroom wall.

Local Connections

Global issues can affect us locally. International free-trade agreements, for example, can result in local price increases and decreases for everything from clothing to vegetables to cars. On the blank spaces provided below, write examples of how global issues could affect people in your locality.

Global Issue	Local Effects
1. World Peace	
2. Trade	
3. Nuclear Energy	
4. Environmental Quality	
5. Hunger	
6. Health Care	
7. Social Policies	

World Traveler

Imagine that you are a member of the U.S. State Department and are about to begin a 30-day fact-finding trip to three regions of the world. You have been directed to write a brief report focused on the following two questions: (1) What stereotypes or misunderstandings do Americans typically have of each of the three regions? and (2) What global issues (such as health, security, natural allocation, economic development, and environmental quality) are prevalent in each of the regions? After you research the three regions, write your answers to these questions on the chart below. You can choose any three of the following regions to research: (1) Latin America, (2) Africa, (3) Middle East, (4) Europe, (5) Russia and other newly independent nations of the former Soviet Union, (6) Asia, and (7) Australia and New Zealand.

Region	Stereotypes/ Misunderstandings	Global Issues

Name _____

What on Earth Do They Do?

Below are listed the names of some important international organizations. Use library resources to research them. Then briefly describe the role of each organization on the lines provided.

1. European Union (EU)

   _____

   _____

2. United Nations (UN)

   _____

   _____

3. Organization of Petroleum Exporting Countries (OPEC)

   _____

   _____

4. International Telecommunications Satellite Organization (INTELSAT)

   _____

   _____

5. League of Arab States (Arab League)

   _____

   _____

6. North Atlantic Treaty Organization (NATO)

   _____

   _____

7. Organization of African Unity (OAU)

   _____

   _____

8. Organization of American States (OAS)

   _____

   _____

   _____

New Symbol

Imagine that you work for a company that manufactures and sells products in locations throughout Europe, North and South America, Asia, and Australia. A decision has been made to replace the company's old logo or symbol with a new one. Employees of the company have been invited to submit designs for the new symbol. The new company symbol must be pictorial, eye-catching, and reflect the company's global dimension. First, give your company a name and identify the product it manufactures and sells. Then, on the space below, draw a design for a new logo or symbol for the company. Be creative!

My company's name is _____.

My company manufactures and sells _____.

Below is my design for the company's new symbol:

Civic Ideals
and Practices

CHAPTER 10
Civic Ideals and Practices

Note to the Teacher: A democratic society cannot function without the participation of its citizens. That is why it is so important to give middle-level students an opportunity to reflect on America's ideals and practices, and then relate them to their own beliefs and behaviors. There are things that all Americans should know about their country and about citizenship. This unit explores citizens' basic rights and freedoms and stresses the important responsibility on the part of citizens to protect their rights and act against injustice.

Unit Goal: The purpose of this unit is to help students explore civic ideals and practices, apply skill in gathering and processing information, and express creative abilities.

Materials: This unit includes the following resources: teacher and student bibliographies, teaching activities, a reproducible student information sheet containing facts, and reproducible student activity sheets for independent study.

RESOURCES
For Teachers:
Goodlad, John, Roger Soder, and Kenneth Sirotnik, eds. *The Moral Dimensions of Teaching*. San Francisco: Jossey-Bass, 1990.

Tindall, George Brown. *America: A Narrative History*. (2 vols). New York: W.W. Norton, 1988.

For Students:
Books
Freedman, Russell. *Lincoln: A Photobiography*. New York: Clarion Books, 1987.

Garraty, John A. *Theodore Roosevelt: The Strenuous Life*. New York: American Heritage, 1967.

Meltzer, Milton. *George Washington and the Birth of Our Nation*. New York: Franklin Watts, 1986.

Meltzer, Milton. *Thomas Jefferson: The Revolutionary Aristocrat*. New York: Franklin Watts, 1991.

Magazines
American Heritage. (Published by American Heritage, 60 Fifth Avenue, New York, NY 10011).

Democratic Ideals
Teaching Activities

Performance Expectations: Students will examine documents that influence America's ideals, analyze the relationship between democratic goals and practices, and analyze qualifications for the presidency.

Preparation: Make individual copies of the "Four Presidents Who Made a Difference" student information sheet and the "Presidential Qualifications" and "Putting Ideals Into Practice" student activity sheets.

Introduction

Ask each student to write down the name of his or her favorite president. As students name their favorites, discuss the reasons for their choices. What qualities do they admire in these individuals? Let the students read silently "Four Presidents Who Made a Difference," which highlights the lives of Washington, Jefferson, Lincoln, and Theodore Roosevelt. Were these four presidents mentioned as favorites by students? If there was room on Mount Rushmore, which U.S. presidents, if any, would they add?

Presidential Qualifications (page 113)

The introductory exercise above should set the stage for this activity. After students individually rank the 20 qualifications, divide the class into groups of four or five students. The groups have a two-fold task. First, students in each group share their individual rankings. Then they try to reach a consensus on a group ranking of the 20 qualifications. After they finish, the groups can share their rankings with the class.

Putting Ideals Into Practice (page 114)

Write the Preamble to the U.S. Constitution on the chalkboard or display it on an overhead projector.

We, the people of the United States, in order to form a more perfect Union, establish justice, insure domestic tranquility, provide for the common defense, promote the general welfare, and secure the blessings of liberty to ourselves and our posterity, do ordain and establish this Constitution for the United States of America.

Probe to see whether students understand the meaning of all the terms in the Preamble. Make certain students realize that the Preamble lists many of the ideals for which our nation stands. Can they cite examples of past government actions that have helped carry out the ideals? After students complete "Putting Ideals Into Practice," let them pair up and compare their responses. Compile a master list of their responses on the chalkboard. From the students' perspective, which ideals have influenced practice in American society the most and the least? Challenge students to identify American ideals found in other sources, such as the Declaration of Independence, Bill of Rights, Mayflower Compact, Emancipation Proclamation, Gettysburg Address, Pledge of Allegiance, and National Anthem.

Four Presidents Who Made a Difference

Carved on the side of Mount Rushmore in South Dakota are the faces of four of America's greatest presidents. Each of them epitomizes civic ideals and practices cherished by Americans for more than 200 years. A few of the deeds and actions of these presidents are recounted below. There are some powerful lessons here about what it means to be an American.

After leading the Continental Army to victory over the British, George Washington was so highly regarded by his fellow citizens that he probably could have been president for life. But Washington had no personal political ambitions and he was against the idea that he should be our country's first president. Only his sense of duty made him change his mind and serve for two terms. In his Farewell Address, Washington spoke of the potential danger of political parties, which he thought might put petty and selfish concerns above the national interest.

"When in the course of human events...We hold these truths to be self-evident...life, liberty, and the pursuit of happiness...we mutually pledge to each other our lives, our fortunes and our sacred honor." The powerful language of the Declaration of Independence reflects Thomas Jefferson's faith in freedom, democracy, and the common citizen. Besides being the author of one of America's most revered documents, Jefferson was a strong advocate of a free press, religious freedom, and public education. Jefferson also initiated America's expansion westward when he secured the Louisiana Purchase and sent Lewis and Clark on their famous expedition across the continent to the Pacific Ocean.

Abraham Lincoln was a homespun man—born in a log cabin and self-educated. But he went on to become the sixteenth president and preside over one of our nation's most profound and tragic events, the Civil War. The conflict arose as an attempt to preserve the Union. The elimination of slavery was never a clear war aim, until Lincoln, in the midst of that great struggle, issued the Emancipation Proclamation. In an "act of justice," he proclaimed that millions of slaves were "...then, thenceforward, and forever free."

Tough-minded and hard-working, Theodore Roosevelt overcame asthma and other serious health problems during his childhood to become one of America's most energetic and effective presidents. Roosevelt was a strong supporter of reform. He broke up the corrupt business trusts, fought for food and drug protection, placed over 150 million acres of forest land in national parks and preserves, and won the Nobel Peace Prize for getting the Russians and Japanese to sign a peace treaty.

These four presidents provided some of the greatest moments in our history. But they are not alone. There are millions of Americans who, day in and day out, do their best for their families, local communities, and the nation. They, too, realize that everything this nation values—peace, democracy, freedom, dignity, justice, equality, life, and liberty—depends upon them.

Presidential Qualifications

The constitutional qualifications for the president of the United States deal only with age, citizenship, and residence. What personal qualifications do you think a U.S. president should have? Below are listed 20 items. Which items do you think should be the most important considerations? Rank the 20 items from "1" for the most important to "20" for the least important. Give reasons for your ranking on the blanks at the right.

Rank   **Reason**

_____ honesty _____

_____ intelligence _____

_____ appearance _____

_____ experience _____

_____ education _____

_____ religious affiliation _____

_____ gender _____

_____ ethnic background _____

_____ position on issues _____

_____ financial resources _____

_____ speaking ability _____

_____ compassion _____

_____ leadership skills _____

_____ integrity _____

_____ toughness _____

_____ core set of values _____

_____ dignity _____

_____ age _____

_____ health _____

_____ decisiveness _____

_____ family structure _____

Putting Ideals Into Practice

Ideals tell us about the way things should be. *Practices* tell us about the way things are. The Declaration of Independence and U.S. Constitution are two major documents that set forth America's ideals. Our nation's history chronicles the progress we have made in putting our ideals into practice. Some important American ideals are listed below. For each of the ideals, circle the one word (*never, seldom, sometimes, usually,* or *always*) that best describes the degree to which the ideal is really put into practice, based on your own observations.

In your opinion, to what degree have each of the ideals listed below influenced the practices of Americans in today's society?

Ideal	**Circle one.**				
1. Peace	Never	Seldom	Sometimes	Usually	Always
2. Equality	Never	Seldom	Sometimes	Usually	Always
3. Democracy	Never	Seldom	Sometimes	Usually	Always
4. Liberty	Never	Seldom	Sometimes	Usually	Always
5. Human Dignity	Never	Seldom	Sometimes	Usually	Always
6. Justice	Never	Seldom	Sometimes	Usually	Always
7. Tolerance	Never	Seldom	Sometimes	Usually	Always
8. Civic Responsibility	Never	Seldom	Sometimes	Usually	Always
9. Freedom	Never	Seldom	Sometimes	Usually	Always

Citizen Action
Teaching Activities

Performance Expectations: Students will gather and analyze information about selected public issues, engage in civic discussions, identify local volunteer groups, and analyze factors that influence foreign policy.

Preparation: Make individual copies of the "Public Issues: Fact or Opinion?" "The Acid Rain Problem: Taking a Close Look," "Campaign Issues," "Changing Foreign Policy," and "Volunteer Groups" student activity sheets.

Public Issues: Fact or Opinion? (page 116)

This activity forces students to discriminate between two types of information: objective, verifiable statements of fact and subjective, unverifiable statements of opinion. Make certain students realize that to think critically about public issues, they must develop informed opinions and correct answers based on knowledge of the facts. Probe to see if students use facts to reach conclusions and formulate possible actions on the issues.

The Acid Rain Problem: Taking a Close Look (page 117)

Let students apply their analytical skills, which should have been sharpened in the exercise above, in an in-depth study of the problem of acid rain. Up-to-date information about acid rain can be found in most world almanacs, as well as in newspapers and magazines. In addition, there are a number of excellent books on the subject for young readers, such as *Acid Rain* by Peter Tyson (New York: Chelsea House, 1992).

Campaign Issues (page 118)

This activity gives students an opportunity to express their creative abilities as they communicate a political message on an issue of their choice. Encourage students to make preliminary sketches of possible posters on scratch paper before committing to a final design. Let them paint, color, or use markers. They can incorporate a scene or symbol into the poster. Display the students' posters on the classroom wall.

Changing Foreign Policy (page 119)

American foreign policy has undergone some significant changes since the stunning collapse of the Soviet Union in 1991. For this activity, encourage students to write to the U.S. Department of State (2201 C Street NW, Washington, D.C. 20520) and ask for information about American foreign policy problems and positions in the seven regions of the world.

Volunteer Groups (page 120)

This activity is designed to help make students more aware of community service work performed by various local groups. After students complete their surveys, challenge them to consider things they can do to improve their community.

Public Issues: Fact or Opinion?

Facts are statements that can be proven to be true. *Opinions* are views that are believed to be true. Research each of the public issues highlighted below. Then list some facts and opinions about each issue in the appropriate boxes.

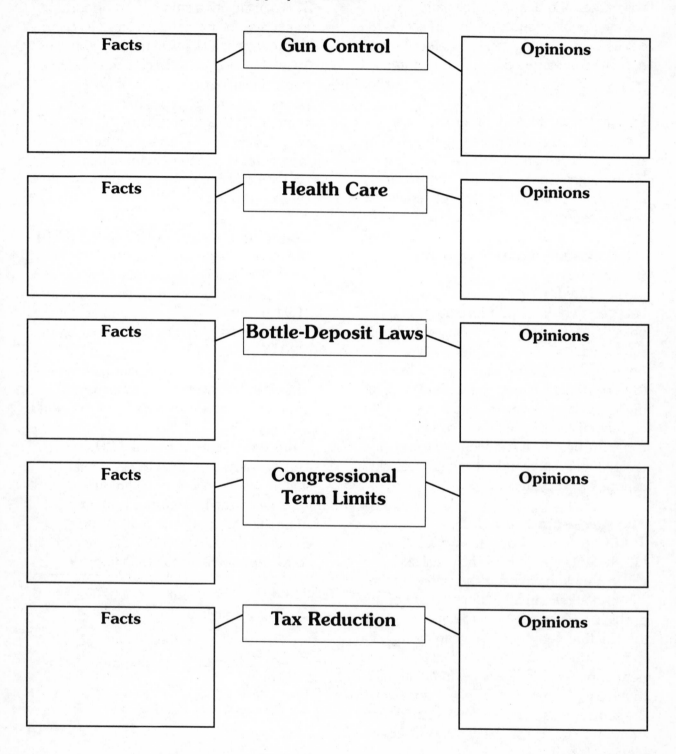

Facts	Gun Control	Opinions
Facts	Health Care	Opinions
Facts	Bottle-Deposit Laws	Opinions
Facts	Congressional Term Limits	Opinions
Facts	Tax Reduction	Opinions

Name _____

The Acid Rain Problem: Taking a Close Look

The Preamble to the Constitution of the United States tells us that one purpose of the federal government is to promote the general welfare. One major threat to the public's welfare is acid rain. *Acid rain*, which is caused by burning fossil fuels, threatens plants, animals, and ecosystems. The world's biggest producer of acid rain is the United States. Investigate the problem of acid rain and find out what the federal government is doing about it. To help you organize your report, answer the questions below.

What is acid rain? _____

_____

_____

What causes it? When did acid rain first become a problem?

_____

_____

Where in the United States is acid rain a problem?

_____

_____

Which animals, plants, and ecosystems have been damaged by acid rain?

_____

_____

Are humans and urban areas harmed by acid rain? _____

_____

_____

How bad is the problem? Is it getting worse? _____

_____

_____

What steps has the federal government taken to deal with acid rain? Has Congress passed any laws? Are federal laws being enforced? Are new laws being proposed?

_____

_____

What are some possible solutions to the acid rain problem?

_____

_____

Campaign Issues

Imagine that you have volunteered to help a candidate run for governor of your state. What key issue do you want your candidate to support? Pick a current issue of concern to the people of your state. Sketch a campaign poster below that shows your candidate's position on the issue. Then create the poster on a larger sheet of paper. Be sure your poster is eye-catching and that its message is persuasive.

Changing Foreign Policy

The nature and purpose of the United States' relations with other nations is called its *foreign policy*. Before 1991, the foreign policy of the United States was based on winning the cold war, which meant stopping the spread of communism supported by the Soviet Union. But two key developments—the breakup of the Soviet Union and the demise of communism— brought an end to the cold war and made the United States change its foreign policy. What foreign-policy problems concern U.S. leaders today? Use library materials and recent information from news sources to identify problems. Then, on the blank spaces below, describe one major foreign-policy problem of concern to the United States for each of the regions of the world listed.

Western Europe

_____

_____

Eastern Europe

_____

_____

Asia

_____

_____

Russia

_____

_____

Middle East

_____

_____

Latin America

_____

_____

Volunteer Groups

Volunteer groups help put civic ideals into practice. Listed below are some of the large national volunteer groups that work to make communities better. On the writing lines, give some examples of the kinds of services provided by each of these groups. There is space for you to list and describe two other volunteer groups in your community. Check the Yellow Pages in your telephone book for a list of local volunteer groups.

American Red Cross

Services provided: _____

_____

_____

Lions Club

Services provided: _____

_____

_____

Kiwanis Club

Services provided: _____

_____

_____

American Cancer Society

Services provided: _____

_____

_____

League of Women Voters

Services provided: _____

_____

_____

Salvation Army

Services provided: _____

_____

_____

Other local volunteer groups:

Group name/Services provided: _____

_____

_____

Group name/Services provided: _____

_____

_____

Answer Key

Chapter 1
Culture

Canadian and American Cultures   page 6
Possible answers include the following:

USA Only
- President is the head of state and the head of government
- Large Asian, Afro-American, and Hispanic populations
- Nation divided into states
- Over 50% of the people are Protestant
- Three separate branches of government

Both Canada and USA
- Celebrate Christmas
- Federal type of government with a constitution
- Political parties
- English is the predominant language spoken (and the official language)
- Celebrate Thanksgiving Day (but on different days)

Canada Only
- Celebrate Boxing Day
- Large French Canadian influence (French is one of two official languages.)
- Nation divided into provinces and territories
- British monarch is the head of state and the prime minister is the head of government
- Constitutional monarchy with a parliamentary type of government
- Roman Catholicism is the largest religious group

Cultural Diffusion   page 8
Silk—discovered in China over 4,000 years ago; source of silk fabric kept a secret from the West for 3,000 years; West traded with China for silk; West discovered the silkworm in A.D. 550; Muslims brought silkworms to Spain and Sicily in the 800s and 900s; by the 1200s, Italy became a silk center; silk weaving spread to France in the early 1500s, and to England in the late 1500s; silk mills were first established in America in 1810.

Glass—first manufactured glass appeared as glaze on ceramic vessels around 3,000 B.C.; first glass vessel appeared in Egypt and Mesopotamia around 1,500 B.C.; blow pipe was invented around 30 B.C. along the eastern Mediterranean coast; by 1291, glass guilds were set up in Venice, Italy; by the 1400s and 1500s, glass technology had spread to Germany and northern Europe; glass technology became important in England during the reign of Elizabeth I (1558-1603); glassmaking first started in America at Jamestown (Virginia) in 1608.

Rubber—European explorers' discovered Indians playing with rubber balls and wearing shoes made of rubber in Central and South America; explorers brought samples of rubber from Peru to France in 1735; in the nineteenth and twentieth centuries, rubber plantations were established in Asia, Africa, and Latin America.

Paper—invented in China more than 2,000 years ago; first used for wrapping not writing; paper industry was established in Baghdad in A.D. 795; paper technology spread to Europe during the Crusades and the Moorish conquest of Spain; first paper mill in America was established in Philadelphia in 1690.

Coffee—discovered in Ethiopia; reached Arabia in the 1200s, then spread from Arabia to Turkey in the 1500s, and to Italy in the 1600s; coffee was brought to Brazil in the 1700s.

Chapter 2
Time, Continuity, and Change

Historical Time   page 19

1492   Columbus reached America
1541   de Soto discovered the Mississippi River
1619   First African slaves came to Virginia
1754   French and Indian War began
1781   Cornwallis surrendered at Yorktown
1804   Lewis and Clark expedition began
1848   California Gold Rush began
1865   Civil War ended
1906   San Francisco destroyed by earthquake
1969   First humans walked on the moon
1992   Bill Clinton elected president

The Meaning Behind the Facts
                                             page 21

1. First successful colony in New England; established a democratic type of self-government that became a model for Massachusetts
2. American colonies declared their right to break away from Britain and form a new nation.
3. Set off an economic boom and revitalized the institution of slavery in the South
4. Convinced southern states to secede from the Union
5. Led directly to the end of World War II and the beginning of the Cold War
6. Led to the decline of world communism and end of the Cold War

Chapter 3
People, Places, and Environments

Exploring Ecosystems   page 29

Some possible answers are shown.

Ecosystem	Locations	Climate	Plants	Animals	Problems
Temperate Broadleaf forest	N. America S. America Europe Asia	temperate	oaks elms beeches	varied	deforestation pollution
Needleleaf forest	N. America Russia, Chile New Zealand Europe Asia	temperate	spruce pines firs	varied	deforestation pollution
Prairie	N. America, Argentina S. Africa Hungary Ukraine	Hot summer Cold winter moderate rainfall	grasses	rabbit, deer mice, foxes prairie dog	overuse
Desert	Africa, U.S. Middle East Asia Australia S. America	dry	cactus shrubs trees grasses	snakes lizards	desertification
Rain forest	S. America Africa S.E. Asia	humid hot	lush green plants tall trees	varied	deforestation
Mountain	Appalachian Rocky Pacific Andes	varied	shrubs mosses trees	goats pikas chinchillas	clear-cutting
Ocean	Atlantic Pacific Indian	surface temp. at poles 28°F at equator 86°F	plankton kelp	varied	pollution

World Landmarks   page 31

1. Great Barrier Reef, Australia
2. Rio de Janeiro
3. Mount Everest, Nepal-Tibet border
4. Grand Canyon, Arizona, USA
5. Victoria Falls, Zambia-Zimbabwe border
6. Nile, Africa
7. Yellowstone, Wyoming, USA
8. Mount Fuji, Japan
9. Amazon Rain Forest, South America
10. Diamond Head, Oahu, Hawaii, USA

Earth Facts   page 33

a. approximately 7,926 miles (equatorial diameter)
b. 5th
c. 3rd
d. 93 million miles
e. revolution or orbit

f. rotation
g. Cancer
h. equator
i. oxygen
j. 71
k. longitude
l. latitude

Capital Coordinates   page 34
1. Athens, Greece
2. Beijing, China
3. Berlin, Germany
4. Jakarta, Indonesia
5. London, United Kingdom
6. Mexico City, Mexico
7. Moscow, Russia
8. Wellington, New Zealand
9. Washington, D.C., USA
10. Ottawa, Canada

Mystery Nations   page 35
1. Germany
2. China
3. South Africa
4. Brazil
5. Canada
6. India
7. Russia
8. Chile
9. Britain

Chapter 5
Individuals, Groups, and Institutions

Groups and Upward Mobility page 60
1. white
2. African-American
3. white
4. 17,803
African-Americans: discrimination, poverty, legacy of slavery
Hispanics: discrimination, poverty, lack of fluency in English

Chapter 6
Power, Authority, and Governance

Checks and Balances   page 66
Legislative Branch:

can impeach the president

approves appointment of judges

can overturn a president's veto

can impeach judges

can declare war

passes laws

regulates trade

can determine the number of justices on the Supreme Court

approves treaties

can propose amendments to the Constitution

approves the appointment of ambassadors

Executive Branch:

signs bills into law

can pardon people

enforces laws

commands the armed forces

can call special sessions of Congress

appoints judges

appoints top members of executive branch

makes treaties with foreign governments

appoints ambassadors

Judicial Branch:

decides on meaning of laws

can declare a law unconstitutional

interprets treaties

Cabinet Departments page 67

1. K		11. G
2. I		12. D
3. L		13. G
4. F		14. B
5. M		15. J
6. H		16. C
7. J		17. J
8. B		18. A
9. E		19. E
10. A		20. C
		21. N

Free Speech and the General Welfare
page 69

Students' opinions will vary. The correct answers are provided for your information.

1. government could restrain free speech because shouting "fire" would create a clear and present danger to people inside the theater
2. burden is on the government to show that a particular song is obscene, violates a person's civil rights, or causes a person to commit a crime
3. under certain circumstances, school officials have a right to limit students' constitutional rights
4. a person who damages another person by what he or she says can be sued for slander

Chapter 7
Production, Distribution, and Consumption

Decisions! Decisions! Decisions!
page 84

1. taxes
2. no
3. $197,120,000,000
4. $337,920,000,000
5. elderly programs, national defense, and social programs
6. Answers will vary.

Chapter 9
Global Connections

Global Rhythms page 103

1. L		11. F
2. M		12. T
3. K		13. P
4. D		14. E
5. O		15. Q
6. C		16. B
7. J		17. A
8. I		18. G
9. R		19. H
10. N		20. S